Teaching Christian Values

Teaching Christian Values

LUCIE W. BARBER

Religious Education Press
Birmingham, Alabama

Library of Congress Cataloging in Publication Data

Barber, Lucie W.
  Teaching Christian values.

  Includes bibliographical references and index.
  1. Christian education.   2. Moral education.   I. Title.
BV1471.2.B357   1984   370.11'4   83-22981
ISBN 0-89135-041-1

Religious Education Press, Inc.
1531 Wellington Road
Birmingham, Alabama 35209
10 9 8 7 6 5 4 3 2

Religious Education Press publishes books exclusively in religious education and in areas closely related to religious education. It is committed to
enhancing and professionalizing religious education through the publication of serious, significant, and scholarly works.

PUBLISHER TO THE PROFESSION

TO
JOHN
CHERISHED COLLEAGUE AND HUSBAND

Contents

Introduction

Values seem to be as elusive as the fictional Scarlet Pimpernel.

We all talk about values. Many of us want to do something about them. But what are they? Religious educators, sociologists, anthropologists, and psychologists have written much about values. Both the man in the street and the woman in the pew are concerned about values. Politicians pay attention to values, and governments are based on values. In fact, the so-called Protestant Ethic (a value set, if ever there was one!) was a basic national value for the first two hundred years of the United States of America.

Nonetheless, we often feel that values are changing. Our national society seems all topsy-turvy. Family life looks like it is going to the dogs. The experience of divorce appears to be all too commonplace. One-parent families continue to increase. Materialism, simple narcissism, and "looking after numero uno" seem to be rampant. If we don't curse the darkness, it gives us a headache.

Increasingly, secular educators are paying attention to what they call values education. In fact, their attention seems to become more and more intense as they are beset by problems of student discipline, juvenile delinquency, and "spaced out" kids. Like all of us, they wonder what is wrong. Like normal humans, they ask whether there is a way out of the seeming social mess in which we find ourselves. Often they also ask about the church's responsibility.

Questions about the social mess that seems to ensnare us all drew me to values education. I have, as a result, looked at values education in secular education and in religious education. Moreover, I have pondered what I saw.

Values may be in shambles: Let us at least admit the hypothesis! Still, a Christian is one marked by the strange sign of hope. Thus, since this is a book about Christian values, it is also inevitably a book about hope. It is a book about what *could* be done about values education within the structures of a Christian religious education. That is why I have divided this book into a sequence of four sections.

In Section I (Values—What Are They?) I plot out the ambiguities that are associated with the central word "values" in chapter 1. Next, I compare the views of religious educators and psychologists in chapters 2 and 3. Finally, in chapter 3 I consider what it could mean to define values as Milton Rokeach does and then state where I stand.

In Section II (How Do We Teach Values?) I consider what is involved in actually setting about to "teach" values. I consider some religious educators who seem to want to teach values in chapter 4 and, in chapter 5, I look at moral education in schools, colleges, and universities. Then, in chapter 6, I try to put all the information together into some fourteen aspects of the "successful" teaching of values.

Since a knowledge of basic human development appears to be important to the "successful" teaching of values, I spend all of Section III on developmental theories. I present nine such developmental theories and in each case seek to relate the theory to the practice of religious education. I quite specifically try to relate each of these nine theories to those fourteen aspects of "successful" values education which I identified in Section II.

In many ways this book could end with Section III. However, I see the first three Sections as but a gateway into Section IV. In this fourth and last section (Seven Christian Values) I consider what would be involved in a life-cycle educational system for "teaching" values within a Christian religious education. For me, that is this book's goal.

Finally, I must enter one caveat. My training has been in an independent college and at a state-supported university. My graduate degrees are in the fields of zoology, education, counseling, and guidance. However, I have always been interested in the art of research and the attempt to improve the human condition. For instance, I spent some eighteen years working for the Character Research Project in Schenectady, New York, where the tradition was activity at the razor's edge between psychological science and religious education. Thus, I approach religious education from a particular perspective. That perspective has permitted me to attempt some things that other, theologically trained religious educators might not have thought of trying. However, I am not really interested in disagreeing with other religious educators. Rather, I believe that I have something to add to a Christian religious education just because of my somewhat different background. I want to complement, assist in the evolution of the field, and, so, cooperate with my colleagues in building toward a better and brighter future by "teaching" what can be called Christian values.

SECTION I

Values: What Are They?

CHAPTER 1

Values and Value Terms

When Benjamin Franklin was twenty-four years old he began a "bold and arduous project of arriving at moral perfection." He made a list of thirteen "virtues" which follows:[1]

1. TEMPERANCE
Eat not to dullness; drink not to elevation.
2. SILENCE
Speak not but what may benefit others or yourself; avoid trifling conversation.
3. ORDER
Let all your things have their places; let each part of your business have its time.
4. RESOLUTION
Resolve to perform what you ought; perform without fail what you resolve.
5. FRUGALITY
Make no expense but to do good to others or yourself, i.e., waste nothing.

6. Industry

Lose no time; be always employed in something useful; cut off all unncessary actions.

7. Sincerity

Use no hurtful deceit; think innocently and justly, and, if you speak, speak accordingly.

8. Justice

Wrong none by doing injuries or omitting the benefits that are your duty.

9. Moderation

Avoid extremes; forebear resenting injuries so much as you think you deserve.

10. Cleanliness

Tolerate no uncleanliness in body, clothes, or habitation.

11. Tranquility

Be not disturbed at trifles, or at accidents common or unavoidable.

12. Chastity

Rarely use venery but for health or offspring, never to dullness, weakness, or the injury of another's peace or reputation.

13. Humility

Imitate Jesus and Socrates.

That is quite a list!

I find two interesting aspects to Franklin's list of virtues. First, Franklin's comments for each virtue suggest a behavioral goal so that he could evaluate whether or not he had *learned* a virtue. Second, Franklin soon discovered that he could work on only one virtue at a time until that virtue became a *habit,* then he could move on to another. Learning a virtue until it becomes a habit implies a learning methodology which Franklin used on himself. He was both teacher and learner.

Virtue

The dictionary defines virtue as "the disposition to conform to the law of right: moral excellence; rectitude," or "the practice of moral duties and the abstinence from immorality and vice."[2]

Plato named four cardinal virtues: prudence, fortitude, temperance, and justice. Christian moralists have added faith, hope, and love.

Virtue is a noun. A person can value a virtue. However, value and virtue are not synonomous. A person can value evil, vice, viciousness, or wrong which are antonyms of virtue.[3] All virtues are values but not all values are virtues. Moreover, Benjamin Franklin portrayed a certain value system when he designated those thirteen virtues as having value for him to learn. These thirteen virtues related to a lifestyle or philosophy of life. Let us inspect those added terms: values, lifestyle, and philosophy of life.

Values

Since values are the main topic of this book, I want to approach a definition gradually. At this point some definitions from the dictionary are appropriate.

"The desirability or worth of a thing; intrinsic worth; utility."[4]
"Attributed or assumed valuation; esteem or regard."[5]
"Rank in a system of classification."[6]

Those definitions are hearty enough. They are very general and certainly any value system would, by common sense, relate to lifestyle or philosophy of life.

What I am attempting to do here is to think of values in a very general sense and then to inspect terms which seem to be related to values. Virtue has been dealt with. Next comes lifestyle.

Lifestyle

The interesting and aggravating thing about the term "lifestyle" is that dictionaries are no help. Look up "lifestyle" or "style, life" and you will find nothing. Yet the term is often used. It is one of those terms, like values, which is widely used by people who assume that, of course, they will be understood. Religious educators are particularly prone to use terms ambiguously. I will illustrate with two examples. Both the religious educators I cite in these examples have a high degree of my respect. In fact they are so well-placed that they can surely take my barbs with equanimity.

James Michael Lee uses the term lifestyle in three different ways: 1) As a behavioral outcome in religious instruction ("performance in a given cognitive, affective, or lifestyle sphere");[7] 2) As a teacher-art of passover ("such a passion can take place on three axes, namely the cognitive, the affective, and the lifestyle");[8] and 3) As a category of instructional contents ("namely product and process contents, cognitive and affective and lifestyle contents, verbal and nonverbal contents").[9] Nine years later Lee added an eighth category ("unconscious content").[10] I have been unable to fathom just what Lee means by lifestyle except for this brief sentence about teacher passover: "The teacher can make the passover by attempting to experience and live in the world just as the learner experiences and lives in the world."[11]

Merton Strommen et al. studied lifestyles.[12] He found "three patterns of behavior": "religious lifestyles, sharing and servicing activities, and questionable moral behavior." Strommen devotes a chapter to religious lifestyles and describes behaviors contributing to religious lifestyles. But he does not define the term. The assumption is made that of course readers will know what is meant by the term. Lifestyle, it would appear, means the way a person lives her/his life, here and now. I will contend that the values a person holds molds, influences, even motivates, a lifestyle.

Philosophy of Life

Here is another term which crops up in religious education and which is ambiguous but frequently used by religious educators.

Philosophy of life is, it seems to me, a term analogous to lifestyle. It may be more sophisticated and/or more all inclusive. Yet in the common genre it inherently makes sense. A person's lifestyle is "managed," as it were, by a higher-level philosophy of life. These are common enough terms, but we can't look them up in a dictionary. I am convinced that lifestyle and philosophy of life are value terms.

There are three people I know of who have studied philosophy of life. Ligon in 1970 defined philosophy of values as "a process of developing value attitudes which increasingly influence one's approach to life."[13] That certainly qualifies on the value dimension. Yet, as a definition it leaves a great deal of ambiguity. What is meant by process? What are value attitudes? What influence is involved? What is meant by approach to life?

Terms shift. Ligon used philosophy of values; Peatling and Tiedeman used only philosophy. Their definition of philosophy is more satisfying: "Philosophy is a complex, organized system of thinking about principles and values, and about their relationship to experiental 'reality.'"[14]

Peatling went on, "Philosophy provides a kind of integration. . . . One's set of basic 'Values' constitutes a subsystem within PHILOSOPHY and, so, is recognized as an important component of an organized system of thought."

Moral Development

Franklin also used the term "moral perfection." Thus, in his mind, Franklin saw a connection between virtues, values, and morals. The term "virtue" is not prevalent today. However, in recent years the usage slipped into awareness when Lawrence Kohlberg asserted that virtue is ultimately one thing, namely "justice."[15] Kohlberg reintroduced "virtues" because he desired to be rid of "a bag of virtues." Virtues are unitary, he proclaimed. "Justice" subsumes whatever is in the bag. Persons develop in their moral judgment based on transitions by stages or levels.

My purpose is not to attack Kohlberg. There are sufficient psychologists doing that. Increasingly religious educators are taking exception to Kohlberg. My purpose is rather to introduce the reader to the breadth of the domain we enter when we talk about values. I started with virtues, then quickly introduced values, value systems, lifestyle, and philosophy of life. Before we knew it we were into moral judgment development, a la Kohlberg.

A religious educator who refutes Kohlberg introduces yet another term, "ethics," particularly "visional ethics," as distinct from "juridical ethics."[16] Craig Dykstra writes, "In juridical ethics, the focus is on making judgments about the rightness and wrongness of particular acts as a judge in a law court might do. The focus in visional ethics is on the way one sees reality and responds to it in the light of that vision."[17] Kohlberg, in his theory of moral judgment development, deals with only juridical ethics. Dykstra, as a religious educator, is "convinced that visional ethics provides a richer, more adequate representation of what the moral life is like for us."[18]

"Our task as moral beings is to be appropriately related to, not just guided by, that center of power and value. Our task is to be obedient to God."[19] Christian values to Dykstra are: 1) the value of being open to revelation, a transformation of imagination,[20] and 2) the value of the disciplines of repentence, prayer, and service. These are the disciplines of discipleship.[21]

Character

The name of Dykstra's book is *Vision and Character*. Character is yet another term to add to our "bag of virtues." "People are unitary beings, and not a cluster of separate, unrelated faculties. The name we give to this unity and the style we have of living as unified beings is character."[22] One's vision shapes one's character. Similarly one's character influences one's vision.

Character education came into religious education by

way of the liberals in the Religious Education Association in the early part of the century.[23] Frederick Tracy in 1922 discussed the meaning of religious education. He wrote "that courses of study should be selected and presented primarily and principally with a view to the making of character and their perfecting of human personality."[24] The early days of REA were highlighted by enthusiasm for the scientific method. Two other endeavors bore the name "character": the Character Education Inquiry and the Character Research Project. The Character Education Inquiry[25] was a huge research effort in the 1920s directed by Hartshorne and May to measure honesty in school children. The Character Research Project, directed by Ernest Ligon, flourished in the 1950s and was "concerned in large degree with traits, such as those reported by Ligon, who made a study of the Christian gospels to derive the characteristics of Christian personality."[26]

Peck and Havighurst speak of "moral character." In fact, in 1960 they proposed a theory of moral development based upon extensive research. Unfortunately their useful theory was eclipsed by all the attention given to Kohlberg. Now we have added moral character and moral development to our "bag of virtues."

Summary

My point is not to keep adding value terms. My point is only to demonstrate what a mixed bag it is. This chapter has been only a first taste. We have briefly inspected virtue, values, lifestyle, philosophy of life, moral development, ethics, character, and moral character. My position is that these are all value terms. Undoubtedly there are other value terms. Further exploration would only add to our confusion. I propose next to continue the exploration into just "values" in order to see whether or not we gain any clarity.

Chapter 1 Notes and References

1. The list of Ben Franklin's virtues appeared in *Ethics in Education,* ed. Donald Craig, Vol. 2(1) (Lunenberg, Nova Scotia, September 1982).

2. These definitions come from the Funk and Wagnalls' *New College Standard Dictionary* (New York: Funk & Wagnalls Company, 1947).

3. Ibid.

4. Ibid.

5. Ibid.

6. Ibid.

7. James Michael Lee *The Flow of Religious Instruction* (Birmingham, Ala.: Religious Education Press, 1973), pp. 45, 272.

8. Ibid., p. 223.

9. Ibid., p. 308.

10. James Michael Lee, "The Authentic Source of Religious Instruction," in *Religious Education and Theology,* ed. Norma H. Thompson (Birmingham, Ala.: Religious Education Press, 1982), p. 116

11. Lee, *The Flow of Religious Instruction,* p. 223.

12. Merton P. Strommen, Milo L. Brekke, Ralph C. Underwager, Arthur L. Johnson, *A Study of Generations* (Minneapolis: Augsburg, 1972), p. 174.

13. Ernest M. Ligon, "A Map for Character Development: Mathematical Group Theory," *Character Potential: A Record of Research,* 5 (1 & 2) (July, 1970).

14. John H. Peatling and David V. Tiedeman, *Career Develop-*

ment: Designing Self (Muncie, Ind.: Accelerated Development Inc., 1977), p. 119.

15. Lawrence Kohlberg, "Stages of Moral Development as a Basis for Moral Education," in *Moral Development, Moral Education and Kohlberg,* ed. Brenda Munsey (Birmingham, Ala.: Religious Education Press, 1980).

16. Craig Dykstra, *Vision and Character: A Christian Educator's Alternative to Kohlberg* (New York: Paulist Press, 1981).

17. Ibid., p. 2.

18. Ibid., p. 3.

19. Ibid., p. 49.

20. Ibid., Chapter 3.

21. Ibid., Chapter 4.

22. Ibid., p. 50.

23. Robert W. Lynn and Elliot Wright, *The Big Little School: 200 Years of the Sunday School,* 2nd edition (Birmingham, Ala.: Religious Education Press, 1980).

24. John Westerhoff III, ed., *Who Are We?* (Birmingham, Ala.: Religious Education Press, 1978).

25. Hugh Hartshorne et al. *Studies in the Nature of Character,* 3 Vols. (New York: Macmillan, 1928–30).

26. Walter Houston Clark, "Research in Religious Education," in *Religious Education: A Comprehensive Survey,* ed. Marvin J. Taylor (Nashville: Abingdon, 1960).

CHAPTER 2

We Are Not Yet Out of the Woods

Not only are there numerous value terms, there are also many ways the term "values" itself is used. In looking at the ways religious educators use the term, I have found five categories: definitions, the place of values in religious education, values-transcendent or immanent, values in evaluation of religious education, and finally, lists of Christian values. The purpose of this chapter is to expose the reader to several examples of each category. The purpose is not to expound on everything religious educators have said about values. That task would be a book in itself. Here, then, are the five categories with examples which will illustrate diversities and seeming disagreements.

Definitions

C. Ellis Nelson, drawing on the work of Clyde Kruckhohn, gives a clear description of values. "First, values are conceptions, that is, they exist in the minds of people."[1] "Second, values are what a person thinks desirable for all people."[2] "Third, values influence action."[3] In another source, Nelson gives a somewhat similar definition. "By values here I mean those attitudes toward himself and others that he voluntarily incorporates within himself and that he believes are desirable for all people."[4] Nelson implies that values influence action within the context of the text from which the second definition was taken. This still leaves the question, are values attitudes or conceptions? Supposedly attitudes are more focused than "the broad generalizations"[5] Nelson attributes to conceptions.

Another religious educator who appears to equate values with attitudes is James Michael Lee. In the "Index to Subjects" in *The Flow of Religious Instruction* the entry for values reads, "Values, 107; see also Attitudes."[6] However, he does make a distinction. "Attitudes are limited to a fairly specific class of objects or persons (such as clergymen or schools or black people) or to an abstraction (such as foreign aid) whereas values encompass generalities."[7] I believe that what Lee means is that "attitudes largely account for a person's approach and subsequent response to values and indeed to most of reality."[8] There is a relationship between values and attitudes.

The next example of a definition comes from the writings of E. Mansell Pattison. "Moral values provide a core of integrative concepts for the development of personality and for the maintenance of society."[9] He further writes about an hierarchy of values from most relative to most absolute: 1) Idiosyncratic values (personal preferences), 2) Group values, 3) Personal values, 4) Operational absolutes, 5) Tentative absolutes, and 6) Permanent absolutes.[10] The

absolutes tend in the direction of universality. The definitions that were mentioned in the first two paragraphs tend
to be definitions of Pattison's personal values 3) or,
perhaps, operational absolutes 4). Pattison adds more
breadth. He also returns us to the idea of conceptions with
his "integrative concepts."

"Values are how we grasp the mixture of good and evil
in any combination of circumstances involving interaction
between ourselves and external reality."[11] Strommen,
Brekke, Underwager, and Johnson hold "that all values
come from the one fundamental idea: good and evil."[12]
Their phrase "how we grasp" suggests that values are a
mechanism. Their more definitive definition follows.
"Values are beliefs held by persons. These beliefs ascribe
relationships between objects and abstract concepts that
sum up to a positive or negative evaluation of a given
object that may be physical, social, or ideal. These evaluations guide selective attention or behavior and impart
moral quality to the process of interaction with the objects."[13] Thus, not only do we add a mechanism, we can
add "beliefs," "evaluation between good and bad," and a
"guide to selective attention or behavior."

The Place of Values in Religion and Religious Education

About the teaching of values, Roman Catholic writers
note, "It is precisely here that Catholic education is most
seriously involved, since its raison d'être is the communication of the Christian understanding of history, doctrine,
and operative Christian values."[14] That is straightforward.
So is the next quotation. "Among Reform Jews, education
has been focused very sharply upon the achievement of

ethical, moral, and religious values."[15] One more example which is straightforward in speaking about religious education: "Since the work of the educator in religion is the direct process of guiding the development of others, it is by nature involved in value building."[16] Religious education, it would appear, is interested in teaching values. This will become clearer (or not so clear?) as we continue with other examples which are not so straightforward as the three above.

Going back into the 1920s, examples can be found regarding values in religious education. Remember that at this time religious educators in the Religious Education Association leaned heavily to personal growth and character education. "Personality and character are looked upon as having inherent and intrinsic value; all other things as having derivative and instrumental value."[17] The student is of highest value and education is to help him toward the ideal which is Jesus' character. Frederick Tracy's refrain from the 1920s is refreshing as is the next example: "Like religion, education is interested primarily in the development of persons and is concerned with the discovery and perpetuation of the highest values of human life."[18] Luther A. Weigle points out that "education is naturally and normally religious." A last example from William Clayton Bower in 1930: Character and religion "are concerned with ethical and spiritual values as the inner motivation and controls of behavior."[19] Thus, religious education is involved in teaching values and, moreover, in teaching the highest values.

One last example for explicating the place of values in religious education comes from Thomas W. Moore. Moore speaks of three levels of learning: 1) conceptual, 2) esthetic, and 3) religious. "Learning which focuses directly on a person's mythic and value orientation and on his experiences of self-transformation is a religious mode of learning."[20] The idea of self-transformation occurs in another example below. The next group of examples speak about the place of values in religion. But implicitly they are related to religious education.

"There are many motives behind the search for religious truth, but probably the ultimate one is the sense of values."[21] Randolph Crump Miller takes a process theology approach to religious education. Value, he writes, "is normally taken to be the equivalent of good."[22] "Religion can be understood in terms of devotion to values."[23] Can we replace "value" with "good"? I suspect that Miller's answer would be, yes. From the Christian point of view religion is devotion to the good or best. However, I still maintain that evil is of value to some nonreligious persons.

Another way to approach Christianity is to speak about religious conversion. V. Bailey Gillespie links conversion with personal identity. "Resolution of the conversion crises of identity will . . . generate values as a product of the experience. One primary function of religion is that of a value genesis. People who know where they fit and who have a new ideology within God's family have a new hierarchy of values, it seems, which aids in the assessments and choices of life."[24] We are reminded here of Moore's "self-transformation."

John Westerhoff well represents religious educators who espouse a socialization orientation. He contends that values are learned in community. "Religious socialization is a process consisting of lifelong formal and informal mechanisms through which persons sustain and transmit their faith (worldview, value system) and lifestyle."[25] He further speaks of two different modes of consciousness:

"responsive-intuitive mode of thinking and the other an active-intellectual mode of thinking."[26] He believes that religious education should pay attention to both modes but mainly to the former. "Values and ethical norms . . . are housed in the responsive mode of consciousness and are intuitive operations of the mind."[27] Thus we add yet another term related to values, responsive-intuitive.

All of these religious educators believe in a relationship between values and religious education. They do not so much disagree with one another. Each has his own orientation and vocabulary. In the next section, we will look at seeming disagreement.

Values—Transcendent or Immanent

Craig Dykstra speaks of mysteries and transcendent realities. The Christian view is "that transcendent centers of value are not only somehow there to be contemplated; they are unified in one Person, an active Power. The Good is not only a value, it is a force."[28]

Randolph Crump Miller writes, "God is not a value, but the primordial nature of God includes the possibility of all values."[29] Good (and by this Dykstra refers to God) is a value. God is not a value. There appears to be a contradiction. However, language can become tricky business when the subject matter is transcendency. Miller posits that his approach to values "leads to a concept of God as a creative entity which creates values."[30] Both Dykstra and Miller believe that values are of God.

That is one side of "seeming dichotomy. The other side is represented by C. Ellis Nelson: "Values are conceptions, that is, they exist in the minds of people."[31] "Values may not be formulated in precise language, but they work incessantly within the mind to shape the thought and action of individuals."[32] Values are in the mind. They are man-made. The transcendent or immanent nature of values is yet another example of different perspectives among religious educators about the term, "values."

Values in Evaluation of Religious Education

We judge people by their deeds. It is also good sense to evaluate people by the values to which they are committed. "How we evaluate ourselves and other people is part of the set of values we use to mark out the meaning of life." Strommen, Brekke, Underwager, and Johnson deliberately used values in their "Study of Generations"[33] along with beliefs, attitudes, and behavior. Some 5000 Lutherans between the ages of 15 to 65 answered a lengthy questionnaire containing 740 questions. This massive study, completed in 1972, is a prime example of values in evaluation. Its purpose was to describe Lutherans and only indirectly to evaluate religious education. Yet the possibility of judging religious education's product is recognized.

"One way to determine religion's success in the world is to observe the deep, ultimate values which it generates and creates."[34] Gillespie gives a clue to the potential of using values in evaluation. "Religious values, like all other values, directly reflect the family's health or pathology."[35] Samuel Natale provides the same clue from a family system approach.

My purpose in this section is not to review research in values. My purpose is only to sketch out the meaning the term values has for various religious educators. There is evidence that religious educators agree that values can be used in evaluation.

Lists of Christian Values

Randolph Crump Miller is among the few religious educators who lists values. He speaks of "lower" values such as bodily, economic, or recreational values. Then there are higher values "such . . . as bravery, wisdom, fullness of life, fidelity, love, and moral greatness."[36] Then, Miller refers to Nicolai Hartman for a group of values which finds "its source in our Christian heritage: steadfast love, truthfulness and uprightness, trust and faith, modesty, humility, aloofness, and sociability."[37] Miller does point out that "values stand in tension with each other. We achieve justice at the expense of mercy and love, purity at the cost of richness of experience, humility at the risk of not asserting our values, sympathy at the expense of honesty."[38]

From Australia comes another list of "central values: love, concern, affection, cooperation, friendship, etc."[39] With the exception of love, this list does not resemble Miller's lists.

Another religious educator who gives us a list is John Westerhoff. His concern is with "the biblical doctrine of shalom (and the metaphor of the kingdom of God)"[40] and religious socialization. Thus, he writes, we "need to explore the values that are inherent in those images, values such as harmony, cooperation, wholeness, nonaggression, unity, corporateness, peace, justice, and concern for the outsider and the oppressed."[41] Here we see some duplication and a number of additions to Miller's and Kleining's lists.

A very general conclusion is that different religious educators value different lists. If one hundred religious educators made lists of Christian values, I suspect we would see one hundred different lists. There would be a great deal of overlap but each lister would have unique values. This attests to the complexity of persons and the complexity of values.

Conclusion

Chapter 1 showed the large number of terms used as value terms. This chapter demonstrates that when looking at just "values" from five points of view, religious educators speak about values in many different ways depending upon their orientation and upon their individuality. We do not find an agreed upon definition. That values have a place in religious education is supported. Yet the place depends upon the writer. There is seeming disagreement about whether values are transcendent or immanent. Perhaps they are both in the sense that man is God's creation. There may be agreement that values are a measure of learning. There may be agreement on some Christian values. But certainly there is no agreement on any particular listing of Christian values.

If we are to teach values in religious education, we need a definition. Then such a definition can help us decide which values to teach. If we are to teach values, the question of transcendent or immanent must be decided in favor of immanence or the venture will not be education. Finally, a curriculum can be decided upon and, as well, evaluation can proceed. We cannot make progress until we have a clear definition. We must know more about values. Perhaps the psychologists can help.

Chapter 2 Notes and References

1. C. Ellis Nelson, "Conscience, Values, and Religious Education," in *Foundations for Christian Education in an Era of Change,* ed. Marvin J. Taylor (Nashville: Abingdon, 1976).

2. Ibid., p. 71.

3. Ibid.

4. C. Ellis Nelson, "Is Church Education Something Particular?" in *Who Are We?* ed. John Westerhoff III (Birmingham, Ala.: Religious Education Press, 1978).

5. Nelson, "Conscience, Values and Religious p. 71.

6. James Michael Lee, *The Flow of Religious Instruction* (Birmingham, Ala.: Religious Education Press, 1973).

7. Ibid., p. 107.

8. Ibid.

9. E. Mansell Pattison, M.D., "The Development of Moral Values in Children," in *Conscience: Theological and Psychological Perspectives,* ed. C. Ellis Nelson (New York: Newman Press, 1973), p. 240.

10. Operational absolutes are "values held by members to be absolute in their application for them." Tentative absolutes are "those operational absolutes found to exist in all societies." Permanent absolutes are "assumptions that may be asserted but unknowable in any scientific sense."

11. Merton P. Strommen, Milo L. Brekke, Ralph C. Underwager, and Arthur L. Johnson, *A Study of Generations* (Minneapolis: Augsburg Publishing House, 1972).

12. Ibid., p. 79.

13. Ibid., pp. 78–79.

14. See "Education to Justice," edited from the *Source Book on Poverty, Justice and Development* by *The Living Light* 10(1) (Spring, 1973).

15. Abraham Franzblau, "Jewish Religious Education," in *Who Are We?* ed. John Westerhoff III (Birmingham, Ala.: Religious Education Press, 1978).

16. V. Bailey Gillespie, *Religious Conversion and Personal Identity* (Birmingham, Ala.: Religious Education Press, 1979).

17. Frederick Tracy, "The Meaning of Religious Education," in *Who Are We?*

18. Luther A. Weigle, "What Makes Education Religious," in *Who Are We?*

19. William Clayton Bower, "A Curriculum for Character and Religious Education in a Changing Culture," in *Who Are We?*

20. Thomas W. Moore, "Religious Education: Third Level Learning," *The Living Light* 10(1) (Spring, 1973).

21. Randolph Crump Miller, *The Theory of Christian Education Practice.* (Birmingham, Ala.: Religious Education Press, 1980).

22. Ibid., p. 115.

23. Ibid., p. 122.

24. Gillespie, *Religious Conversion and Personal Identity*, p. 212.

25. John H. Westerhoff III and Gwen Kennedy Neville, *Generation to Generation* (Philadelphia: United Church Press, 1974).

26. John H. Westerhoff III, "Values for Today's Children," *Religious Education* 75(3) (May–June, 1980).

27. Ibid.

28. Craig Dykstra, *Vision and Character* (New York: Paulist Press, 1981).

29. Miller, *The Theory of Christian Education Practice*, p. 126.

30. Ibid., p. 117.

31. Nelson, "Conscience, Values, and Religious Education," in *Foundations for Christian Education in an Era of Change*, p. 71.

32. Ibid.

33. Strommen et al., *A Study of Generations.*

34. Gillespie, *Religious Conversion and Personal Identity*, p. 157.

35. Samuel M. Natale, "A Family Systems Approach to Religious Education and Development," *Religious Education* 74(3) (May–June, 1979).

36. Miller, *The Theory of Christian Education Practice,* p. 125.

37. Ibid., p. 125.

38. Ibid., p. 125–126.

39. John Kleinig, "The Place of the School in Moral Education," *Journal of Christian Education,* Papers 73 (April, 1982).

40. Westerhoff and Neville, *Generation to Generation,* p. 131.

41. Ibid.

CHAPTER 3

Can the Social Scientists Help?

"Value. Quantitative measure in terms of some standard or unit." That is all the help we get from Drever's "A Dictionary of Psychology."[1] Values defined in that way remind us of the price tags in the supermarket. Yet values are standards. Ernest Hilgard writing about adolescents says, "If the adolescent is to achieve any consistency in his social behavior, he has to arrive at standards of conduct. He must decide for himself the kind of person he wishes to be and ascertain for himself what things are worthwhile. Such standards are known as ideals or values."[2] Values are ideals and standards by which to evaluate worthiness.

"Human behavior is partly governed by value preferences and self-evaluative standards."[3] Albert Bandura is writing about values and personal standards which influence the associates and environments we choose. "Chance encounters" are those situations over which we have no control. However, in plotting our future paths, we can somewhat control our futures through the mechanism of our values. This casts yet another light on the meaning of values and suggests a motivational aspect for values.

"A value . . . is an imperative to action . . . is a standard or yardstick to guide actions, attitudes, comparisons, evaluations, and justifications of self and others."[4] Milton Rokeach in 1968 put it all together. Or so it seems.

In 1971 A. H. Maslow made this statement: Values "are defined in many ways and mean different things to different people. As a matter of fact, it is so confusing semantically that I am convinced we will soon give up this catchall word in favor of more precise and more operational definitions for each of the many submeanings that have been attached to it."[5] Two illustrations may suffice to demonstrate Maslow's meaning. Muzafer Sherif and Hadley Cantril were interested in ego-involvement. "Values are the chief constituents of the ego."[6] They contrast "social values" with "personal values" and thus begin their own values terminology. Morris Rosenberg is a Self psychologist who does not use Sherif and Cantril's vocabulary. "By self-values we refer to conceptions of the desirable which serve as standards or criteria for self-judgment."[7] It is not that these psychologists ultimately disagree with each other. They just have different ways of using the term *values.*

Thus, as with religious educators, psychologists perceive of values in different ways. Instead of continuing to confuse the reader, I am going to now begin to build the case for how I understand values. I will do this by reviewing the psychologists with whom I am most comfortable in the area of personal and social values.

As a beginning, there are two general uses of the term "values." The term can be used about a person who values or about an object which has value. I will be using the first sense exclusively. My interest is in the values people hold.

B. F. Skinner rejects the notion that people hold values. People are reinforced: "The reinforcing effects of things are the province of behavioral science, which to the extent that it is concerned with operant reinforcement, is a science of values."[8] I am not that extreme a behaviorist and wish to study what is in the black box, the mind.

G. W. Allport defined *values* as "a belief upon which a man acts by preference."[9] He is the Allport of Allport, Vernon, and Lindzey that we associate with the *Study of Values*. Brewster Smith defined *values* as the "conceptions of the desirable that are relevant to selective behavior."[10] The definition of *value* which is more clearly thought-out is that of Milton Rokeach.

Rokeach

A *value* is an enduring belief that a specific mode of conduct or end state of existence is personally or socially preferable to an opposite or converse mode of conduct or end state of existence.[11]

That definition includes Allport's and Brewster's definitions and expands them. Let us first look closely at Rokeach's definition. By labeling values as enduring, Rokeach is not saying that values are stable. "If values were completely stable, individual and social change would be impossible."[12] Values do change. But there is an enduring quality to them which saves us from chaos. The values we learned as young children most likely are with us today, perhaps modified.

Rokeach calls a value a belief. However, not all beliefs

are values. There are three types of beliefs: "descriptive or existential beliefs, those capable of being true or false; evaluative beliefs, wherein the object of belief is judged to be good or bad; and prescriptive or proscriptive beliefs, wherein some means or end of action is judged to be desirable or undesirable. A value is a belief of the third kind—a prescriptive or proscriptive belief."[13]

As with all beliefs, values have cognitive, affective, and behavioral components. A person can think cognitively about a value. A person can feel affectively about a value. And a "value has a behavioral component in the sense that it is an intervening variable that leads to action when activated."[14]

Now to deal with *modes of conduct* and *end-states of existence.* Rokeach refers to two kinds of values, *instrumental* and *terminal.* Terminal values represent end-states of existence such as salvation, freedom, and peace. Instrumental values represent modes of conduct by which end-states are achieved. Forgiving, responsibility, and loving are instrumental values.

Rokeach makes further distinctions which may clarify values for religious educators. He distinguishes two kinds of terminal values: personal values and social values. Salvation and peace of mind are personal, while world peace or brotherhood are social. We speak of both kinds of values in religious education. Rokeach divides instrumental values into two kinds: moral values and competence values. Moral values have an interpersonal focus. Their violation leads to feelings of guilt. Competency values are personal in focus. Their violation leads to feelings of shame about self-inadequacy. "Thus, behaving honestly and responsibly leads one to feel that he is behaving morally, whereas behaving logically, intelligently or imaginatively leads one to feel that he is behaving competently."[15] Religious educators dealing with whole persons should recognize both moral values and competency values. Persons who feel incompetent or self-inadequate are handicapped in activating their moral values.

The word "preferable" remains to be clarified in Rokeach's definition of values. Notice that he does not use "conceptions of the desirable." He uses a predicate adjective which specifies that something is preferable to something else. One mode of conduct or end-state is preferable to an opposite mode or end-state. This is much stronger than, "I prefer cereal for breakfast," or "I prefer the red dress."

There is another sense in which Rokeach uses "preferable." "A person prefers a particular mode or end-state not only when he compares it with its opposite but also when he compares it with other values within his value system. He prefers a particular mode or end-state to other modes or end-states that are lower down in his value hierarchy."[16]

Rokeach's definition of a value system "is an enduring organization of beliefs concerning preferable modes of conduct or end-states of existence along a continuum of relative importance."[17] Now we begin to explore Rokeach's theory of a system of beliefs more thoroughly. The value system is central to the overall belief system. We can start at the periphery of the belief system. Here we find tens of thousands of beliefs. Several beliefs can be organized to form a single attitude. Then two or more attitudes can be organized to form an attitudinal system. (A religious ideology is an attitudinal system.)[18] Attitudes are functionally and cognitively connected to a few dozen instrumental values which, in turn, are functionally and cognitively connected to even fewer terminal values. The core of the whole system of beliefs is the self or self conception. Values maintain and enhance self- esteem. "Values are standards that tell us how to rationalize in the psychoanalytic sense, beliefs, attitudes, and actions that would otherwise be personally and socially unacceptable so that we will end up with personal feelings of morality and competence, both indispensable ingredients for the maintenance and enhancement of self-esteem."[19]

Since Rokeach's meaning of values is appropriated for the rest of this book, let us dig a little deeper. Attitudes and values are both beliefs. But what is the difference between an attitude and a value?

"An attitude is a relatively enduring organization of interrelated beliefs that describe, evaluate, and advocate action with respect to an object or situation, with each belief having cognitive, affective, and behavioral components."[20] Persons have as many attitudes as they have had encounters with specific objects or situations. Values are more general and are not related to specific objects or situations. Values are standards. Attitudes are not standards. Values are motivational. Attitudes are motivational only in the sense that they serve in the achievement of one or more values. Values involve ego defense and self-actualizing functions. Attitudes involve such functions only inferentially as they relate to values.

Rokeach proclaims that values are more central than attitudes. Whereas his initial reputation was gained by studying attitudes, Rokeach now champions the study of values as the proper domain of social scientists. It is more economical to study values because people have only a few values and tens of thousands of attitudes. Since values determine attitudes and behavior, values are more important to study. Rokeach explains why in the past so many studies about attitudes were made. The reason, quite simply, was that scientists knew how to measure attitudes. They did not know very much about measuring values.[21]

Measuring Values

An early attempt to measure values is known today after several revisions as the Allport-Vernon-Lindzay *Study of Values*. Six values are measured: theoretical, economic, aesthetic, social, political, and religious. Although this tool has been used in close to a thousand research studies, questions remain. Does it cover all values? Does it merely measure superficial interests?[22]

Another instrument was devised by Sundberg, Rohila, and Tyler in 1970. The Sundberg-Tyler (S-T) Values Q-sort assumes that "values are possibility-processing structures."[23] The seven-step Q-sort uses fifty statements of "personal assumptions" and forty statements of "personal directions." This is somewhat like Rokeach's terminal and instrumental values. However, the S-T Values Q-sort has not been as widely used as Rokeach's *Value Survey*. Thus more is known about the *Value Survey*.

The *Value Survey* has eighteen instrumental values and eighteen terminal values printed on separate, removable gummed labels. The testee's value system is revealed by rank ordering the items in each of the two sets. A most important value is peeled off and placed in Box 1; a next most important value is peeled off and placed in Box 2 and so forth until all eighteen boxes of a set are filled. Corrections and/or revisions are easily made.

Rokeach originally collected values from philosophers,

students, and adults whom he interviewed. His final lists are the following:[24]

Terminal Values	Instrumental Values
A Comfortable Life	Ambitious
An Exciting Life	Broadminded
A Sense of Accomplishment	Capable
A World of Peace	Cheerful
A World of Beauty	Clean
Equality	Courageous
Family Security	Forgiving
Freedom	Helpful
Happiness	Honest
Inner Harmony	Imaginative
Mature Love	Independent
National Security	Intellectual
Pleasure	Logical
Salvation	Loving
Self-Respect	Obedient
Social Recognition	Polite
True Friendship	Responsible
Wisdom	Self-Controlled

In 1968 the *Value Survey* was administered to a national sample of 1409 men and women by the National Opinion Research Center.[25] Other information was gathered at the same time so that the researchers could compare the value systems of males and females, rich and poor, educated and uneducated, old and young, and more. Studies were made on race, on political values and on religious values. I will only summarize here the findings on religious values.

"Two values—*salvation* and *forgiving*—stand above all the others as the most distinctively Christian values."[26] Jews and nonbelievers rank *salvation* last. Jews place higher value than do Christians on *equality, pleasure, family security, inner harmony, wisdom* and, also, *capable, independent, intellectual,* and *logical.* One surprising result was that "there is no evidence from the national sample that being *loving* and *helpful* are distinctively Christian values."[27] Christians rank these two values the same as non-Christians. Perhaps Christian educators should teach the values of being *loving* and *helpful.* But how does one teach values?

Chapter 3 Notes and References

1. James Drever, *A Dictionary of Psychology* (Baltimore: Penquin Books, 1952).

2. Ernest R. Hilgard, *Introduction to Psychology* (New York: Harcourt, Brace & World, Inc., 1962).

3. Albert Bandura, "The Psychology of Chance Encounters and Life Paths," *American Psychologist* 37(7) (July, 1982).

4. Milton Rokeach, *Beliefs, Attitudes, and Values* (San Francisco: Jossey-Bass, Inc., 1970).

5. A. H. Maslow, *The Farther Reaches of Human Nature* (New York: The Viking Press, 1971).

6. Muzafer Sherif and Hadley Cantril, *The Psychology of Ego-Involvements* (New York: John Wiley & Sons, Inc., 1947).

7. Morris Rosenberg, *Conceiving the Self* (New York: Basic Books, Inc., 1979).

8. B. F. Skinner, *Beyond Freedom and Dignity* (New York: Alfred A. Knopf, 1971).

9. G. W. Allport, *Pattern and Growth in Personality* (New York: Holt, Rinehart and Winston, 1961).

10. M. B. Smith, "Personal Values in the Study of Lives" in *The Study of Lives,* ed. R. W. White (New York: Atherton, 1963).

11. Milton Rokeach, *The Nature of Human Values* (New York: The Free Press. A Division of Macmillan Publishing Company, 1973).

12. Ibid., p. 5.

13. Ibid., p. 7.

14. Ibid., p. 7.

15. Ibid., p. 8.

16. Ibid., p. 10.

17. Ibid., p. 5.

18. Rokeach, *Beliefs, Attitudes, and Values*, p. 163.

19. Rokeach, *The Nature of Human Values*, p. 13.

20. Rokeach, *Beliefs, Attitudes, and Values*, p. 132.

21. Ibid.

22. Leona E. Tyler, *Individuality* (San Francisco: Jossey-Bass Publishers, 1978).

23. Ibid., p. 142.

24. Rokeach, *The Nature of Human Values*, pp. 357–361.

25. Ibid., p. 82.

26. Ibid.

27. Ibid., p. 83.

SECTION II

How Do We Teach Values?

CHAPTER 4

Religious Educators and Values

"It is clear that the family is the foundation of religious education and values."[1] Samuel Natale suggests family field trips, parents' groups, and the development of resource materials and advice for parents. Since Peck and Havighurst's pronouncement about parents' influence on the children in their families,[2] religious educators for the most part are convinced that parents somehow pass on their values to little children. How do parents pass on their values? Psychologists are apt to talk about *identification, introjection,* and *internalization.* However, Winifred Hill prefers the language of social learning theory and uses terms like *primary reinforcement, secondary reinforcement,* and *vicarious reinforcement.*[3] Kohlberg uses *cognitive structural development.* Wilcox adds *social perspective.*[4]

Ways of Teaching Values

Rather than becoming mired down in terms again, I propose to address teaching values by categorizing ways of

teaching values into three groupings of curriculum theories. Robert Newton proposed three groups of curriculum
theory as the Individual Fulfillment School, the Scholarly
Discipline School, and the Behaviorist School.[5] First I will
describe these schools and then illustrate each by examples
of religious educators and their advice.

Individual Fulfillment. In this category the aim of religious education is "to be and become."[6] The student is
given rich resources by a teacher who is a facilitator-part-
ner. The student is at the center of a process for the "natural discovery of God within."[7] The advocates of this position are experientialists, personalists, and open educators.

Scholarly Discipline. The aim in this category is "to
know."[8] The teacher becomes the "mediator of the religious subdisciplines"[9] (scripture, historical theology, systematic theology, religious morality, religious ritual). The
student is a "beginning practitioner of the religious subdisciplines"[10] on the road to "scholarly understanding of
religious phenomena."[11] Advocates of this position are
theologians.

Behaviorist. The aim in this category is "to do."[12] The
student responds to a "reinforcing religious environment,"[13] while the teacher is the "structurer of a reinforcing religious environment."[14] The student adapts to the
"systematic development of religious attitudes and knowledge."[15] Advocates of this position are "social science"
methodologists.

At this point I am not advocating one of these "themes"
over against another theme. Nor am I suggesting that
these three themes are all-inclusive for the purpose of
teaching values. I am heading into a discussion of the art
of how religious educators propose to teach values, and
without some organization the ways, at least to me, are

staggering. Thus I have, for the time being, chosen Newton's three themes or categories around which to initiate discussion.

Finally, a caveat. When I choose a religious educator to illustrate one of the three themes (or categories) I do not forever after lock her/him into that category. Personally, I would be distressed if I were identified as *only* a Behaviorist. I think of myself that way, to be sure. At the same time, I also think of myself as belonging to the Individual Fulfillment School and the Scholarly Discipline School. For the time being, I will identify religious educators in one or another category for convenience in illustrating themes.

Individual Fulfillment

The first example of the Individual Fulfillment School is V. Bailey Gillespie. Gillespie is a religious educator from the West Coast whose recent book, *Religious Conversion and Personal Identity*,[16] reveals the author's competencies in both theology and psychology. He is chosen to represent the Individual Fulfillment School because of his chapters on religious instruction and counseling. Here is how Gillespie would teach values.

In the first place, a questor-guide relationship needs to be established. "It would be well for leaders and youth to function together as units, sharing roles and experiences of faith and understanding mutual identities, rather than adults trying to manipulate youth to accomplish conversions or to 'have' an experience."[17] Gillespie objects to teachers who feel they must be in charge or who feel they know what is best. Such an authoritative approach cripples youth's creativity. Religious educators should demonstrate an "openness for questioning."[18] They should "reflect the God they too seek."[19] They should avoid preaching and be able to "listen to counter arguments."[20] They should provide "an atmosphere of trust, hope, and fidelity in which youth could select the direction of their lives."[21]

The climate of the educational setting is important in the learning of values. Gillespie suggests "informal discussions," "retreats," "value orientations among various disciplines within our churches," and "meeting for direction with all the individuals involved in worship, where God can minister to the school by his Spirit."[22]

Gillespie promotes the use of Scripture, not passages that merely "inform and clarify. . . . But in such passages as invitations to disciple, to find one's sense of history, to commitment and to change in lifestyle."[23]

Thus, the teacher provides rich opportunities to challenge learners in their quest for values. The teacher/counselor's "role must be that of helping guide and assist in the struggle, rather than giving out information in pat answers."[24] The learner is the center of the educative process. The teacher is the facilitor-guide.

Another religious educator who illustrates the Individual Fulfillment School is Craig Dykstra. Dykstra's concern is with moral education. His conception of morals is not limited to Rokeach's instrumental values of the moral type. Due to Dykstra's orientation in visional ethics, he is interested in teaching the Christian values of repentance, prayer, and service.[25]

Dykstra believes that moral education can occur only in a moral community. "The community as a whole is the essential context for Christian education for the moral life . . . the character of that community determines greatly the kinds of experience we can have there."[26] A community wrapped up in self-service and bare maintenance cannot be an educational environment for learning Christian values. But the community is not everything. There must be teachers. And teachers of a very special kind. "The primary and basic act of the teacher must be to be receptive, attentive, and present to the learners." "The teacher must be capable of being available as a servant to the learner; and this is only possible to the degree that the teacher is free to refrain from manipulating the student in some way to enhance the teacher's own self-establishing and self-sustaining mechanisms."[27] This is more than modeling a moral life for students. A relationship of mutuality is needed which is initiated by the teacher and accepted by the student.

In introducing students to the disciplines of discipleship, the teacher must first discover the problems with which each learner is struggling. Next the teacher must provide "resources that will help the learners explore the dimensions of these struggles." Dykstra mentions biblical resources for "the learners to read, ponder, explore, and discuss." Church history, biographies, "novels, plays, poetry, music, and art forms can also be very helpful."[28]

A third step is for the teacher to provide "actual encounters between the persons in conflict."[29] Field trips, interviews, and counseling relationships are strategies that are useful. The teacher must help the learner in interpreting such encounters. "As much as it is the teacher's responsibility to guide the explorations of the learners, the teacher does not and cannot pretend to do the exploration for the learners."[30] "What we hope for, as teachers, are insights, understandings, and actions that arise out of the learners from their own repentance, prayer, and service."[31]

Learning of this kind cannot be rushed. "The fourth

step in the teaching-learning process is to provide time and space for students to struggle on their own, and to take time out from their struggles with the encounters they have had and the guidance they have received."[32] Dykstra faults Values Clarification and the Kohlbergian approaches to moral education for pressuring learners into premature commitments.[33]

The final step for Dykstra is interpretation. "The role of the teacher at this point is to listen, to suggest possibilities of interpretation in expression and action—all, of course, in the context of a relationship that is deeply respectful of the learner's own insights and styles of interpretation, and without self-serving motivation on the part of the teacher."[34]

Both Dykstra and Gillespie appear to belong to the Self-Fulfillment School of curriculum theory. We move on to the Scholarly Discipline School.

Scholarly Discipline

As a theologian, Randolph Crump Miller is an example of the Scholarly Discipline School. "Theology clearly determines to a great degree the content of Christian education. What we teach depends on what we believe."[35] In addition to the discipline of theology, Miller would "make use of the insights of educational psychology, the sociology of learning, and cultural anthropology."[36]

The subdisciplines Miller would have learners become practitioners in are: doing theology, worshiping, appreciating more and more values, and understanding the Gospel message. He emphasizes "knowledge of the data, development of Christian character, and life within the fellowship of the church."[37]

Miller is scholarly. However, his theories put to practice need not produce scholars. His focus is on relationships, the relation between God and learner and between learner and others in a faithful community. Whereas Gillespie and Dykstra talk mostly about educating youth, Miller constantly talks about all age levels from birth to adult maturity. He discusses the importance of the family. "What happens in the first three years of a child's life is a determining factor for future religious development."[38] He writes about worship for all ages and the use of the Bible for all ages. The scope of Miller's thinking surely cannot be entirely contained in the Scholarly Discipline School.

Just as Miller cannot be contained wholly in the Scholarly Discipline School neither can the cognitive developmentalists. Mary M. Wilcox is a good example of the cognitive developmentalists in religious education.[39] Her work focuses attention on how people make meaning. The subdisciplines of interest are Logical Reasoning, Social Perspective, and Moral Reasoning (a la Kohlberg), and a, so far, minor subdiscipline, Role of Symbols (a la James Fowler). Wilcox's students are early practitioners of these subdisciplines, but at a developmental state where each is. A Stage 1 learner is stimulated only to Stage 2. A Stage 2 learner is stimulated only to Stage 3. Developmentalism is certainly within the assumptions of the Scholarly Discipline School, but in religious education, according to Robert Newton, a first principle is "scholarly understanding of religious phenomena."[40] Wilcox reminds her readers that the learner is a whole person. "I want to stress that behavior, emotions, moral and logical thinking, and imagination and intuition are all parts of the same journey. No part can be exchanged for another, nor can a person function effectively without development in each part."[41] Nonetheless the "piece of pie" she picks out is largely cognitive.

She rejects three contemporary responses to values education: 1) "Leave values education to the home and church,"[42] 2) "Teach the traditional values on which everyone agrees,"[43] or 3) "Help each person to discover what his or her own values are, making no judgments about them."[44] She opts for a "fourth response: a model for teaching the whole person."[45]

She promotes six elements basic to her fourth response: 1) "Information must be available to the learner." 2) "The instructor needs to be aware of the manifestations of developmental theory." 3)"Feelings play a critical role in learning." 4) Learning involves both rational functions and imagistic functions of the mind. 5) "The learner seems to require active physical involvement for optimum learning to take place." And, finally, 6) "Learning is facilitated by the support of a community."[46]

The reader is already aware that both Miller and Wilcox, although having some common identities with the Scholarly Discipline School, also have common identities with the Self-Fulfillment School. We shall soon see that they also share with the Behavioristic School. Examples of the Behaviorist School come next.

Behaviorist

Robert Newton, who proposed the three schools of curriculum theory I have used (for the sake of organizing this chapter), felt that he had a prime example for behaviorist theory. "The application of the behaviorist theory to religious education has recently been proposed in quite explicit terms."[47] His candidate is James Michael Lee which probably is no surprise to anyone, although Lee certainly does not consider himself as a behaviorist. I am not too sure about the "quite explicit terms." If one were to explore the specific Skinnerian approach in religious education, I believe that you would see differences between the so-called *social science* approach (Lee's) and *programed instruction*. Programed instruction has been tried in religious education.[48] But it is not the same thing as the social science approach. However, if Newton, who translated secular categories over into religious education categories, was not precise, I am willing to follow his lead *only* because he has given me a way to organize.

Lee, to be sure, concentrates on behavioral objectives. He would appear to classify the teacher as a "structurer of a reinforcing religious environment."[49] He might think of the curriculum as "precise objectives, careful strategy for producing the desired knowledge and attitudes."[50] In Lee's words "teaching is that orchestrated process whereby one person deliberatively, purposively, and efficaciously structures the learning situation in such a manner that specified desired learning outcomes are thereby acquired by another person."[51]

"Attitudes largely account for a person's approach and subsequent response to values and indeed to most of reality."[52] Thus, what Lee has to say about teaching attitudes is germane to values education. Every teaching-learning interaction is a complex process involving teacher, learner, subject-matter content, and environment. Teaching attitudes is no different. Lee gives us four clues. "First, the teacher should consciously and deliberatively teach for attitudes."[53] Attitudes can and must be taught. "Second, the teacher should put the student in a learning situation which is concrete and which contains many first-hand experiential variables."[54] This is an example of deliberately involving teacher, learner, subject-matter content, and environment in interaction in concrete experiences. "Third, the teacher should so structure the concrete learning situation that it features considerable interpersonal interaction among the members of the learning group."[55] He suggests role playing when interpersonal experience must be contrived. "Fourth and finally, all the variables in the total educational environment must be deliberatively targeted toward the learning of values."[56] It is not enough to teach values in a classroom if those values are not supported throughout the school.

Lee maintains that there are three times in life when values education is most appropriate: early childhood, adolescence, and young adulthood. The most important time is in early childhood. Therefore, Lee advocates close cooperation between religious educators and parents (young adults) of young children (birth to six).[57] Thus values education can focus on two crucial periods in life at the same time. In fact Lee insists upon the "importance of the family as the primary agent of religious instruction"[58] of which values are an essential part.

Another religious educator who is interested in teaching values and in the importance of family is John Westerhoff. "The church has always maintained that religious education begins in the home through the imitation of parents and participation in family and community worship."[59]

Westerhoff's approach to teaching values is through socialization. As far as I can ascertain, a socialization approach belongs to the Behaviorist School, rather than to the Self-Fulfillment School or the Scholarly Discipline School. There is a certain amount of *rearranging the environment* involved, particularly as Westerhoff wants to *hurry up* socialization. "We need consciously, purposefully, and continuously to act so as to force social change to occur."[60] I do not believe that Gillespie, Dykstra, Miller, Wilcox, or Lee would disagree with Westerhoff's position. Their means would be different, to be sure. But what are Westerhoff's means? How would he teach values?

"We are socialized into our beliefs, attitudes, and values."[61] By this Westerhoff means that children imitate parental behaviors in their struggle to adapt to society's values. In sorting out behaviors which are acceptable and/or unacceptable, children experiment in order to find behaviors which are reinforced or not reinforced. The structure of the family and the family child-rearing practices are all important. Indian families, where the family structure is multigenerational and living is communal, pass on values to their children of cooperation and nonaggression. Texas homesteaders, whose family structure is based on carving out a homestead, transmit to their children the values of competition, independence, and aggression.[62]

Westerhoff's goal in hurrying up socialization is the formation of Christian communities supporting families in their socialization of their children. His interest on the one hand is the promotion of Christian values as found in the Gospel and on the other hand in seeking ways to transmit these values in today's changing forms of family structures. He gives five guidelines:

> We need to tell and retell the biblical story—the stories of the faith—together.
> We need to celebrate our faith and our lives.

We need to pray together.

We need to listen and talk to each other.

We need to perform faithful acts of service and witness together.[63]

Westerhoff wants to replace the school paradigm with the "community of faith-enculturation paradigm."[64] He wants to move away from the teacher-learner model so dear to James Michael Lee in religious instruction. Rather, Westerhoff believes that the method of education is interaction where the distinction of teacher-learner is of least importance and thereby obliterated. "Shared experience, storytelling, celebration, action, and reflection between and among equal 'faithing' selves within a community of faith best helps us understand how faith is transmitted, expanded, and sustained."[65] To Westerhoff that "is the best way to understand educational method in a faith community."[66]

One of the interesting consequences of using Newton's Categories of Curriculum Theory to organize this chapter is to put Lee and Westerhoff into the same category. I suspect that neither of them would have considered themselves in one category although I hope I am wrong. However, I would like to use this opportunity to make a supplemental comment.

Both Lee and Westerhoff are artists in religious education. Both want to educate for Christian values. Both want to advance the expertise of the art. Yet they are very different as they paint their pictures of religious education. Both paint on large canvases. Lee paints a macrotheory. Westerhoff paints a vision. I believe their difference lies in the brush strokes each applies. Lee paints in fine brush strokes whereas Westerhoff uses large brush strokes. Lee's painting pays attention to detail. Westerhoff paints more for impression. Lee is a precise Seurat whereas Westerhoff is a dazzling Van Gogh. I believe that religious education needs them both.[67]

Both Lee and Westerhoff believe in the importance of early childhood in the learning of values. Both believe in parenting education. Lee paints in the details of the teaching-learning process, while Westerhoff paints the dynamic mural labeled "socialization."

Conclusion

We have looked at six religious educators and how each would teach values. Gillespie and Dykstra have much in common and fit well the Individual Fulfillment School's description. Miller and Wilcox are very different and do not fit well the Scholarly Discipline School's descriptions. Lee and Westerhoff have little in common with each other or with the other four and do not fit comfortably in the Behaviorist School. Gillespie and Dykstra focus on adolescents and youth. The other four focus on the lifelong teaching of values and all call attention to value learning of the very young child and the importance of parenting in values education.

I have only touched on Values Clarification. Both Wilcox and Westerhoff make use of Values Clarification techniques, but only for their own perceived purposes and to clarify Christian values, not any relativistic values. Values Clarification will be inspected in the next chapter where we will be concerned with how secular educators teach values. Can secular educators add methodologies not found in this chapter?

Chapter 4 Notes and References

1. Samule M. Natale, "A Family Systems Approach to Religious Education and Development," *Religious Education* 74(3) (May–June, 1979).

2. Robert F. Peck and Robert J. Havighurst, *The Psychology of Character Development* (New York: John Wiley & Sons, 1960).

3. Winifred F. Hill, "Learning Theory and the Acquisition of Values," in *Psychological Studies of Human Development,* ed. Raymond G. Kuhlen and George G. Thompson (New York: Appleton-Century-Crofts, 1963).

4. Mary M. Wilcox, *Developmental Journey* (Nashville: Abingdon, 1979).

5. Robert R. Newton, S. J., "Current Educational Trends and Strategies in Religious Education," *Religious Education* 67(4) (July-August, 1972).

6. Ibid., p. 258.

7. Ibid.

8. Ibid.

9. Ibid.

10. Ibid.

11. Ibid.

12. Ibid.

13. Ibid.

14. Ibid.

15. Ibid.

16. V. Bailey Gillespie, *Religious Conversion and Personal Identity* (Birmingham, Ala.: Religious Education Press, 1979).

17. Ibid., p. 208.

18. Ibid., p. 210.

19. Ibid.

20. Ibid.

21. Ibid., p. 211.

22. Ibid., p. 216.

23. Ibid., p. 219.

24. Ibid., p. 228.

25. Craig Dykstra, *Vision and Character* (New York: Paulist Press, 1981).

26. Ibid., p. 124

27. Ibid., p. 125.

28. Ibid., p. 130.

29. Ibid.

30. Ibid., p. 132.

31. Ibid., p. 132.

32. Ibid., p. 133.

33. Much the same point about giving adolescents unpressured time is made by Lucie W. Barber in "The Dichotomies of Thinking and Feeling," *Religious Education* 76(5) (September-October, 1981).

34. Dykstra, *Vision and Character,* p. 134.

35. Randolph Crump Miller, *The Theory of Christian Education Practice* (Birmingham, Ala.: Religious Education Press, 1980), p. 176.

36. Ibid., p. 177.

37. Ibid., p. 159.

38. Ibid., p. 283.

39. Wilcox, *Developmental Journey.*

40. Newton, "Current Educational Trends and Strategies in Religious Education," p. 258.

41. Wilcox, *Developmental Journey,* p. 23.

42. Ibid., p. 184.

43. Ibid., p. 185.

44. Ibid., p. 186. (Wilcox discusses her objections to Values Clarification.)

45. Ibid., p. 188.

46. Ibid., pp. 189–190.

47. Newton, "Current Educational Trends and Strategies in Religious Education," p. 257.

48. For a review of work in programed instruction by re-

ligious educators, see John H. Peatling, *Religious Education in a Psychological Key* (Birmingham, Ala.: Religious Education Press, 1981), chapter 8.

49. Newton, "Current Educational Trends and Strategies in Religious Education," p. 258.

50. Ibid.

51. James Michael Lee, *The Flow of Religious Instruction* (Birmingham, Ala.: Religious Education Press, 1973), p. 206.

52. Ibid., p. 107.

53. Ibid., pp. 116–118.

54. Ibid., pp. 116–118.

55. Ibid., pp. 116–118.

56. Ibid., pp. 116–118.

57. Another advocate of this position is the author. See Lucie W. Barber and John H. Peatling, *Realistic Parenting* (St. Meinrad, Ind.: Abbey Press, 1981).

58. Lee, *The Flow of Religious Instruction*, p. 64.

59. John H. Westerhoff III, *Bringing Up Children in the Christian Faith* (Minneapolis: Winston Press, 1980), p. 7.

60. John H. Westerhoff III and Gwen Kennedy Neville, *Generation to Generation* (Philadelphia: Pilgrim Press, 1974), p. 169.

61. Ibid., p. 153.

62. Ibid., chapter 7.

63. Westerhoff, *Bringing Up Children in the Christian Faith*, p. 36.

64. John H. Westerhoff III, *Will Our Children Have Faith?* (New York: Seabury, 1976), p. 50.

65. Ibid., p. 88.

66. Ibid.

67. In the past Lee has consistently placed himself in opposition to Westerhoff. See his chapters in *Religious Education and Theology*, ed. Norma H. Thompson (Birmingham, Ala.: Religious Education Press, 1982) and *Moral Development, Moral Education, and Kohlberg*, ed. Brenda Munsey (Birmingham, Ala.: Religious Education Press, 1980). However, a more conciliatory

Lee appears in a recent chapter in Kevin Walsh and Milly Cowles' book, *Developmental Discipline* (Birmingham, Ala.: Religious Education Press, 1982). Perhaps these two artists can appreciate one another.

CHAPTER 5

Moral Education in the Secular Domain

We concluded chapter 4 on how religious educators teach values with John Westerhoff as an example of a socialization approach. I cannot agree wholeheartedly that Westerhoff belongs to a Socialization School. He orients himself to an anthropological perspective. Yet he is too impatient to wait for social change. The term socialization implies nonintentionality. But, Westerhoff, as an educator, is intentional.[1] And he is intense in the way a muralist is intense.

Before getting any further into this chapter, I would like to make one more point about the Socialization School in religious education with Westerhoff as an example of what I wish to illustrate. The idea comes from the generative work of John H. Peatling in religious education.[2] Peatling makes an important distinction between socialization and education, particularly religious education. The distinction has to do with closed-ended systems vs. open-ended systems. Socialization tends to be closed-ended with a focus on what is and has been. Education, certainly religious education, in the mainline Protestant denominations and Roman Catholicism, tends to strongly associate with open-ended systems. The emphasis is not only what is but also what can be. John Westerhoff is a prime example of what is but also what can be. This is the vision of a muralist.

Moral education in the secular domain is education, not socialization. It is intentional and it is open-ended. The development of healthy personalities and good citizens is moral education's objective. I plan to begin this chapter with a discussion about Values Clarification. Then, I will describe other moral education programs.

Values Clarification

Louis Rath, Merrill Harmin, and Sidney Simon wrote the book, *Value and Teaching* in 1966.[3] They were concerned with the emotional health of children, particularly those with behavior problems. They felt that children could be helped if they knew clearly what values they stood for. Without advancing any specific values, the authors instituted a methodology to help children choose values freely, consider alternatives and consequences of the alternatives, begin to cherish their values, affirm them publicly, and act on them consistently. The methodology was called Values Clarification. The methodology consists of exercises or strategies such as Values Voting, Values Continuum, and Rank Orders which stimulate students to clarify their values. Most exercises are fun. The methodology quickly gained popularity across the country. More exercises were added[4] and Values Clarification became merged with Humanistic Education[5] in the schools and character-building agencies.

While Values Clarification treats values as relativistic, the methodology did and does have an advantage over moral development strategies. All values, instrumental and terminal, are fair game. General values, and these would include Rokeach's personal and competency values, are considered. For example, a sentence completion exercise might include stems such as "I am happiest when. . . ." or "I'm best at. . . ."

The relativism of Values Clarification is bothersome to both religious educators in Christian values education and secular educators involved in citizenship education.[6] Both religious and secular educators have specific values in mind which they want to teach. The rationale involved for both is that institutions (both church and schools) have a hidden curriculum. Specific values are taught, perhaps unconsciously, but they are taught. Therefore, educators can and should teach specific values purposively, values which are appropriate to the given institution.

The relativism charge is not the only objection to Values Clarification. James S. Clinefelter and Charles R. Knicker raise the issue that "students may be stating values they presume the leaders or their peers expect them to have."[7] This is a rather serious charge.

Two other charges against Values Clarification are brought up by Mary Wilcox.[8] Wilcox points out that in a Values Clarification mode a group of sixth graders may decide on a value where they are developmentally. For example, the acceptability of lying about their age in order to see a movie. If the teacher believes that such a response is dishonest, she/he has a dilemma. Values Clarification is nonjudgmental. Everyone's values are of equal worth. Is this religious education?

Wilcox's second objection has to do with the question of using gimmicks with students who soon become jaded with fun and games.

Another charge against Values Clarification comes from a Jewish religious educator. Joseph Lukinsky wrote an article titled "Two Cheers for Values Confusion." His point, as I see it, has to do with pushing decision makers into value decisions before they are really ready. A mature commitment to live a religious life involves struggling with the tension between self values and the religious community's values. Values Clarification glorifies "self-development from within" and in Lukinsky's view is too simplistic. "Confusion should be nurtured. It is the enemy of smugness, of seeing oneself as the measure of all things."[9]

John L. Harrison, a Canadian professor of education, wrote an appraisal of Values Clarification in which he gives a lengthy description of the methodology and the background for that methodology. His final conclusion is that "Values Clarification methods are found to rest on untried empirical assumptions and seriously insufficient theoretical foundations."[10] An equally harsh judgment comes from empirical research on curriculum effectiveness. James S. Leming reviewed thirty-three studies during the past fifteen years which meet a criterion of replicability in the classroom. His conclusion was, "The research on Values Clarification indicated that little or no confidence is warranted regarding its potential curricular effectiveness."[11]

And yet, Values Clarification continues to thrive. I know of at least five centers or institutes which promote Values Clarification.[12] A recent book is titled *Turning Points: New*

Developments, New Directions in Values Clarification.[13] Kirschenbaum links Values Clarification with civil liberties, which is an important aspect in secular education. "Not only is values clarification consistent with the principles of civil liberties, it helps teach and reinforce them."[14] Thus, Values Clarification is not likely to disappear, particularly in public schools. The strategies are generally popular if they are not overused. And the strategies, themselves, can be used in teaching specific values.[15]

Moral Education

Values Clarification is, of course, a part of Moral Education. But Values Clarification can be treated separately because it does not espouse particular values and because it is not based upon developmental theory. Other Moral Education programs do espouse particular values and are based on one or more developmental theories. In fact, the number of developmental theories involved includes social perspective theory, psychoanalytic theory, ego theories, structural cognitive theories, and emotional development theory. Lawrence Kohlberg is very prominent. But the names of Hogan, Selman, Loevinger, Sprinthall, Mosher, and others are also important.[16]

I rather doubt that many religious educators appreciate how large the movement is for Moral Education in the secular domain. Some figures will give an idea of the activities in recent years. The journal *Moral Education Forum* publishes an annual bibliography of new books, articles in journals, and abstracts of doctoral dissertations. In 1979 there were 36 new books, about 200 articles and 62 dissertation abstracts.[17] In 1980 there were 47 new books, about

300 articles and 62 abstracts.[18] And in 1981 there were 19 books, 254 articles and 64 abstracts.[19] In addition, in 1981, 6 bibliographies for Moral Education were announced.[20] These figures give a picture of Moral Education activities in this country. Great Britain publishes *The Journal of Moral Education*, which is an international journal.[21] JME publishes accounts of Moral Education in Great Britain and other countries, both East and West, North and South. Moral Education programs flourish around the world.

My problem is how to introduce this large body of literature. Obviously, I can do no more than make an introduction or provide a way to get in the door. If you are convinced, as I am, that religious education must include Values Education, then you will have to go through the door more completely. The least I can do is give you a floor plan of the house you will enter. The basement and first floor will be for preschool and elementary school ages. The second floor will be for junior high and senior high-school ages. The top floor will be for college ages, with a small attic for adults. The rooms at each level will be small or large depending upon the number of strategies that are carried out simultaneously and the number of developmental theories that are the bases for each program.

I am not attempting to give a full description of the house, Moral Education in the Secular Domain. That can be found elsewhere.[22] I can only give a brief description of the rooms with illustrations of programs with which I am acquainted.

Preschool: The Foundation Level

Most discussions about Values Education programs or strategies are organized chronologically beginning with

Blatt's intervention in the 1960s and moving sequentially through the 1970s and 1980s.[23] I am going to take a different route. My highway begins, in the basement, with a preventative mode. Values Education programs at the preschool level have the purpose of teaching values early in order to stave off future problems. At the elementary-school level, or the first floor of our house, we find a mixture of preventative and remedial programs. Then at the secondary level, or the second floor, we find more and more remedial programs because junior highs and senior highs often suffer from mixed values or contradictory values. The Values Education movement started in secondary schools. It started in a remedial mode. After more than ten years of persistent effort, there are many programs on the first floor and a few in the basement where prevention is the mode.

One of the ideas that has filtered down from the secondary level is the idea of a just community.[24] However, Suzanne L. Krogh[25] has pointed out that Montessori preschools were actually, from the beginnings in 1907, training grounds for a just community. The basic idea of the method was to prepare the environment and to give presentations of the learning materials to each of the children individually with the aim of having them learn to work independently at their own speed. Thus they learned independence. There was a mix of ages in the classroom. Thus the older children learned to help the younger children. There was no make-believe equipment. Rather the children learned by using the real articles. Thus the children learned to care about their environment and to use the learning materials in the proper way, with care and respect. The children learned self-discipline as they worked and learned within their community. "Her belief that prior to the age of six this development was directed by 'an unconscious power' which no adult could force, led Montessori to let the children create their own community through providing them with an environment dedicated to growth in freedom for each child."[26]

Today there are many preschools throughout the country using the Montessori method.[27] They represent one room in our house's basement. There is another basement room which is completely different. It is a home-based program. The children are taught values of positive self-regard. The teachers are their parents who learn the principles of *Realistic Parenting* in group meetings with other parents.[28] The parents learn about child development so that they can assess their child's level of development and set realistic goals to teach one higher level. The parents learn skills to stimulate their child to try a new behavior which they can then reinforce. Through the child's actions, the child learns foundational attitudes such as the value of purposiveness, persistence, cooperation, sociability, and imagination. Such a firm foundation prepares the children for entering the world of formal schooling. Both the Montessori preschools and *Realistic Parenting* are proactive and preventative.

Whereas the Montessori preschools are based on her theories of child development and pedagogy, the *Realistic Parenting* program is based on the theories of Piaget, Peatling,[29] and B. F. Skinner. No mention has been made of Kohlberg at the preschool level. However Kohlberg will be prominent on the first floor of our house, the elementary school level.

The Elementary School Level

I am going to describe eight rooms on this floor. Kohlberg's stages of moral judgment development are featured in most of these rooms. Therefore, here is a brief description of the three stages which appear at the elementary level. Bear in mind that Kohlberg declares that these stages are invariant and sequential and that they represent cognitive structure.

Stage 1. Obedience and punishment orientation.
Children at this level respond to rules and labels of good and bad or right and wrong. They are concerned about how authority figures will react and about whether children will be punished or rewarded.

Stage 2. Naively egoistic orientation.
Children at this level realize that right action is that which is self satisfying and occasionally satisfying of others' needs. They believe one good turn (or bad deed) deserves another.

Stage 3. Good-boy orientation.
Children at this level want approval and want to please and help others. They conform to majority norms. Intention becomes important for the first time.[30]

Movement from stage to stage is stimulated by the experience of moral conflict, discussion of different points of view and exposure to moral reasoning at a next higher stage. That is why we will be seeing the use of discussion so prevalent in all of the rooms we will be entering.

The first room we will enter is the Selman and Lieberman Room, named after the investigators who planned the program.[31] The class of second graders meets twice a week for a half hour to forty minutes. They watch a sound filmstrip about a moral dilemma and then enter into a discussion which stimulates them to consider moral reasoning a stage beyond their present stage.

In the second room, the Biskin and Hoskisson Room, much the same thing is going on, except now we are in a fourth and fifth grade classroom.[32] There are no sound filmstrips. Instead, the class looks at moral dilemmas found in children's literature as a lead-in to discussions.

Next we go into an entirely different room, the Enright Room #1.[33] These are first-grade pupils with their specially trained teachers. The teacher's training is in social cognitive development. Kohlberg doesn't enter into this classroom, except that Enright is well aware of Kohlbergian theory. Something else is going on here. The values taught in this room have to do with development in friendship skills[34] and the social problem-solving skills.[35] Yes, there are classroom discussions of social problems each week. Yet, the real crux of the matter has to do with the children's everyday, so-called discipline problems. Jimmy hits Billy. The teacher asks feeling questions of each. "How do you feel about what happened?" "How do you think Jimmy (Billy) feels about what happened?" These are questions to stretch development to a next higher friendship level. "What else could you have done in this situation?" This is a question to stretch development in social problem solving—the consideration of alternative behaviors. Pupils are faced with their present problems and asked to reflect on their solutions. Quite simply put, it is an action-reflection model. In contrast to the first two rooms, the problems are not hypothetical or contrived. The problems are the children's everyday classroom problems.

Now, as we go on to five more rooms, you will see elaborations of these first three rooms. The elaborations will be in the number of strategies and the number of developmental theories involved. We will tend to be talking about values teaching in the upper elementary level.

The fourth room is the Ostarch Room.[36] The twist in this fifth-grade classroom is that a trained high-school senior is the teacher. Her training is in leading discussions about a moral dilemma with the younger children. Her goal is to facilitate the children's thinking and discussing together. The student teacher presents the class with a dilemma. Then the students are polled about what X should have done. Next, small group discussion occurs followed by class discussion. Finally, the forty-five minute class period is concluded with decision making. Of course in this cross-age situation, not only are fifth graders encouraged in social perspective taking and working through a problem, the high-school senior is engaged in personal growth in psychological education.[37]

The Grimes Room[38] has something added which is innovative and successful. The mothers joined their fifth and sixth grade children in trying to solve moral dilemmas. They found the moral dilemmas in a novel appropriate for fifth and sixth graders. Next they wrote out moral dilemmas of their own and even presented dramatizations of their vignettes. Compared to a student-only group and a control group, the children-with-mothers group gained significantly more on Kohlberg's Moral Judgment Scale.

What other innovations can we find? Let us go into the Wallin Room.[39] Here are sixth and seventh graders enrolled in a creative dramatics course. Selman's theories of peer interaction is the basis of the program. The pupils dramatize moral dilemma situations in small groups. The dramatizations were all videotaped, played back to the class, and then discussed. Commerically available materials were used at first.[40] After several weeks the children created their own dilemmas and dramatized them. Thus, they started with hypothetical situations but then began working on problems from their own experience.

The Enright Room #2[41] has another cross-age component. Sixth graders are trained to lead small groups of first graders in discussion of moral dilemmas. Commercial filmstrips are used to stimulate discussion. The sixth graders meet once a week with the first graders. They also meet once a week in the sixth-grade class for a period with their trainers to reflect on their experiences with the younger children. We saw this action-reflection model in the Enright Room #1. However, that was a first grade only program. The focus in Enright Room #2 is on the development of sixth graders.

The last room at the elementary level is the Sullivan Room.[42] Actually the Sullivan Room is a house in itself with ethical education going on K–12. This is the Ethical Quest Project in Tacoma, Washington. It involves forty-three elementary schools, ten junior high schools and five high schools. There are several interesting things about the Ethical Quest Project which can be helpful for religious educators.

1. Since the project directors knew that teaching of values was involved, they gave a great deal of time well-spent in obtaining community support. They worked closely with community advisory boards and their school board. They paid attention to spreading information widely.

2. A great deal of time was spent in teacher training. The teachers were trained in developmental theory, in how to identify moral issues in existing curriculum and how to deal with day-to-day moral issues as they arise naturally.

3. The final curriculum was not added on to existing courses. The teachers studied existing materials and wrote their own curricular materials.

4. Supervision was available to the teachers and supplementary training was also available to the teachers.

The strategies employed in Project Quest included: "individual reading, class discussions, role-plays, writing assignments, interviews of adults and other students, debates and class meetings."[43] For example an elementary school unit is on rules. The pupils are given a list of school rules and then challenged to think about what a principal, a teacher, and a parent might say about each rule. By role-playing, children are encouraged to look at others' points of view. This social perspective taking ability is essential to intellectual and moral development.

Project Quest is based on the work of Piaget, Kohlberg, Selmen, Loevinger, and others. The Sullivans "tried to stimulate students to move from limited, egocentric thinking to autonomous principled thought."[44] The project combines both a preventative orientation and a remedial orientation. The project has goals for the students' personal growth and also the learning of citizenship values.

Junior-High and Senior-High Level

I could take you room by room at this level. But what you would see is a good deal of what you saw on the first floor. You would see moral dilemma discussions prompted by commercial materials, by filmstrips, by audio-visuals, and by literature or present-day life problems. You would see role-playing and dramatizations. You would see parent involvement. After all, this is the level where moral education all began. It began in the remedial mode. Secondary schools in the 1970s were jungles of drug abuse, materialism, narcissism, vandalism, and delinquency. The problems demanded remediation.

Values clarification was and is an attempt at a remedy. Moral education based on Kohlbergian theory was another attempt at a remedy. Something had to be done in education to get us out of the mess we were in. Junior-high and senior-high schools were the environments where problems first showed their nasty heads. The modern day Values Education started at this level in order to solve problems.

The history of Values Education today goes back only fifteen years or so. It is interesting how quickly remediation at the secondary level filtered down into the elementary level and took on a preventative mode. During those initial fifteen years another thing happened which is important to note. Values Education at the secondary level ceased being the application of band-aids and began the patient, long-term process of a more preventative orientation.

In describing the second floor of moral education in the secular domain, I want to take you into two new rooms. The eight rooms we visited on the first floor are here on the second floor, to be sure. But it is the new rooms that are enticing. The two new rooms are: Psychological Education and the Just Community. I have mentioned both before. Now we can inspect each of these rooms in more detail. There is an aspect of remediation in both these rooms. But there is also a healthy dose of prevention and proactive theory involved. Students are learning values in order to be better prepared for the future. The values, of course, are citizenship values as they must be in the secular domain. Our interest in this chapter is with the strategies for teaching values. Can religious education profit from the strategies used in secular society?

Psychological Education

Psychological education, or developmental education as it is also called, was first announced in 1970 in an article in *American Psychologist* by Ralph Mosher and Norman Sprinthall.[45] These authors were steeped in the philosophy and theories of John Dewey. Moreover, they had access to the research findings in recent years on developmental stages. They work around the stage theories of Piaget on cognitive development; Kohlberg, on ethical development; Loevinger on ego development; and Selman on interpersonal development.[46] We will be dealing with descriptions of stage theories in the second half of this book. Suffice it to say here that knowledge of the learner's stage of development can indicate to the teacher the appropriate learning environment which the teacher can provide. For example, if the learner is at Kohlberg's Stage 3, good-boy orientation, the teacher provides an environment to challenge movement toward Stage 4, authority- and social-order-maintaining orientation. We saw on the first floor, the elementary-school level, how challenges are managed. Moral dilemma discussion was a main strategy. Role-taking and cross-age tutoring are other strategies.

However, Mosher and Sprinthall have a broader view of education than only development in moral judgment. They conceive of the whole person who is the learner. They seek to develop the potentialities of the learner's self within self and without self in interpersonal relationships. This more total psychology about the learner is a reason for the label, psychological education.

Most of the programs in psychological education that have been tried by Mosher and Sprinthall and/or their students have followed an action-reflection model. One such program will illustrate. Philip Cognetta and Norman Sprinthall worked with high-school students in a special social studies class. The senior-high students were trained in teaching techniques so that they in turn could teach junior-high school students. The classroom teacher demonstrated teaching skills to the seniors. Then the class members tried the skills on each other, critiquing each other. Twice a week the senior-high students taught small groups of junior highs. Then each week they had a seminar to debrief, watch video tapes of their teaching behaviors and reflect upon their progress. The practicum-seminar balance continued for twelve to fourteen weeks. Students showed increased stage scores in ego-development and moral reasoning; thus, moving them to greater psychological maturity.[47]

While psychological education programs have as their aim the psychological maturity of individuals, another effort aims at creating a "just community" with a group in schools.

Just Community

In the mid-1970s a more comprehensive effort began in moral education programs. The educational leaders realized that any institution has a hidden curriculum in teaching values because of the school's administration and staff. How can students be expected to learn fairness if the teachers hold all the power? How can students appreciate justice when the school's disciplinary structure is not just? These same questions can be asked by religious educators. How can learners learn to love in a community which is not loving? How can they learn mercy in a community which is unforgiving?

Attempts at forming a just community were started in Cambridge and Brookline, Massachusetts and in Pittsburgh, Pennsylvania. The Cluster School under Kohlberg took place in Cambridge.[48] Mosher led the School Within a School in Brookline.[49] The Carnegie-Mellon Civic Education Project in Pittsburgh was directed by Edwin Fenton.[50] In each of these projects a selected student body spends time as a community within the larger, entire student body of the school. Students take special courses of the psychological education type described above. Teachers are open and fair in classrooms. Perhaps the most outstanding feature in all three projects is the Town Meeting as it is called in Brookline's School Within a School. Town Meeting meets once a week. Each person, whether student or teacher, has one vote. The Town Meeting decides how the community will be organized and run. Students learn the values of democracy by participating in a democratic community.

The formation of a just community does not happen overnight. In fact, appreciable results were not realized until the end of the second year in the above mentioned projects. There must be substantial teacher training. Students need time to develop psychologically.

Instead of describing in more detail the three projects, I am going to describe the Scarsdale Alternative School's *Just Community* (S.A.S.).[51] S.A.S. benefited from Kohlberg's, Mosher's, and Fenton's experiences in starting their own just community in 1977. Staff members became immersed in cognitive moral theory at Kohlberg's Institute for Moral Education at Harvard University. Theory helped teachers understand the developmental level(s) of students and, of course, their own developmental level, which does not necessarily match the students' level(s).

Teacher training at the Institute consists of a thirty-hour graduate course taught over four weeks in the summer.

"In implementing the *Just Community* in Scarsdale, great attention was paid to staff development and, to some extent, the implementation of structural changes was ensured because the development of these structures was a product of the faculty and students working together rather than having these structures imposed upon them."[52] Thus, the adults in any community must be well-prepared to work *with* students.

S.A.S. also prepared its students. The academic year begins with a two-week orientation program. "Students are introduced to the ideology of the school and provided with opportunities to practice participatory skills. Task groups are established, which tackle recurring school problems. Interspersed with these are a variety of cooperative group games and activities."[53] Two weeks taken away from academic studies seems an expensive luxury. But it is deemed essential for getting the just community off to a good start.

Once a week, throughout the school year, a community meeting is held for one-and-a-half hours. Everyone is required to attend and everyone has one vote. Community meetings are the governing body of S.A.S.

Also, once a week each student participates in a core-group meeting with ten or twelve students and a teacher/advisor. These meetings are held in a home in order to encourage close relationships between members. Here such subjects as drugs, stealing, loyalty, and infringement of rules are discussed.

S.A.S. also has a fairness committee which represents the community in a rule-enforcing function and also in a function of helping to resolve interpersonal disputes.

There are two courses at S.A.S. which are deliberately prepared for moral education goals. These are "Ethical Issues in Decision Making" and "Taking a Stand: An Argumentative Writing Curriculum." These courses help the class: 1) Confront a moral dilemma, 2) Have students state a position, 3) Test the reasoning for positions and 4) Adopt a final position.[54] These steps are also followed more informally in all classrooms whenever a moral dilemma is encountered.

That is but a brief description of Scarsdale's just community. However, it gives you an idea of how seriously some schools consider the importance of value education. The values are values of a good citizen in a democracy run for justice.

College Level

There are only two projects in values education that I know of which are going on at the college level.[55] They are the Sierra Project at the University of California, Irvine, and the values education curriculum at Alverno College in Milwaukee, Wisconsin.

Sierra Project

The Sierra Project involves residential living experiences as well as academic experiences. It is a just community on a grander scale than the high-school just community projects. Hear John Whiteley, the director of the Sierra Project: "The Sierra Project, in its efforts to raise the level of students' moral reasoning, is more similar to psychological education approaches than to moral education approaches. Rather than teaching developmental theory or introducing systematic exercises presenting artificial moral dilemmas, we used those moral dilemmas which arise from the natural living experiences of the residence hall."[56]

Sierra Hall is one of many residence halls on the campus of the huge University of California, Irvine. Sierra Hall houses fifty students. In order for students to be accepted for residency in Sierra Hall, students must enroll in the class, *Social Ecology 74: Moral Development and Just Communities*. Sierra Hall residents may also elect a "two-unit laboratory course . . . which involves working at least five hours per week in a paraprofessional counseling or service role in the surrounding community."[57]

Hours in the special class or in the laboratory class are few compared to the twenty-four hours a day living in the community of Sierra Hall. In order to facilitate community living, each student in Sierra Hall belongs to a Triple I-D group made up of eight freshmen and one sophomore student staff member. The Triple I-D stands for "Intensive Interpersonal Interaction and Discussion."

The core curriculum of the academic course on Moral Development and Just Communities includes modules on "empathy/social perspective-taking, community building, sex-role choices, assertion training, community service, conflict resolution, and race roles."[58] Other modules are reserved for sophomore, junior, and senior classes.[59]

I have mentioned the sophomore student staff in the Triple I-D groups. They act as "peer advisor; teaching assistant, peer counselor; teaching aide, participant-observer; role model, and friend."[60] They live in Sierra Hall and are on the firing line twenty-four hours a day. The professional staff teach the academic classes. Their role with the students in the classroom shifts from the fall term, to the winter term and to the spring term. In the fall term, freshmen seem to need high structure in the course work, students' tasks are explicitly defined. This emphasis shifts in the winter term as teachers teach skills of assertion, socialization, sex role, life and career planning. "In the spring quarter, the role of the teacher is to directly encourage students to assume responsibility for thinking about what they are learning."[61] Teachers are trained as psychologists and teach accordingly. Their aim over the freshmen year is to develop students as active learners for the remaining college years in values education.

The Sierra Project is an amazingly complex project. Only the freshman year has been described here. The whole project is considered as character education. Thus, it involves students as psychological wholes. The theoretical bases are Kohlberg's moral judgment theory, Loevinger's ego-development theory, and theories from counseling psychology, particularly Mosher and Sprinthall's work. The Sierra Project began in 1975 and continues into the 1980s.

Alverno College

Alverno College is a liberal arts college for women. There is a heavy emphasis on experiential learning which is implemented by "mastery learning" or "outcome-centered" curriculum.[62] Eight outcomes[63] include a valuing ability which is broken down into a "learning sequence of six increasingly complex levels."[64] The following are the six levels for the valuing ability:

Identifying own values

Inferring and analyzing values in artistic and humanistic works

Relating values to scientific and technological developments

Engaging in valuing in decision making in multiple contexts

Analyzing and formulating the value foundation of a specific area of knowledge, in its theory and practice

Applying own theory of value and the value foundation of an area of knowledge in a professional context[65]

Students are required to complete the first four levels, and they may or may not work on levels five and six. Students contract with faculty to work on a level. They must be credentialed by faculty as having achieved a level before they can work on a next higher level.

"Each faculty member analyzes his/her course and decides where and in what ways the course contributes most naturally to the development of the valuing ability and how student achievement of the competence can best be demonstrated and assessed."[66] In any particular semester about half the faculty in all academic departments are teaching toward the valuing ability.

There is a Valuing Competence Division which supervises the effectiveness of teacher strategies. For example, they assess the effectiveness of moral dilemma discussions for stimulus potential to challenge moral growth. The Valuing Competence Division also assesses the individual student's progress and gives feedback to the students on their progress.

Each spring students are interviewed in order to check on their perceptions of their developing abilities. Students write essays on their values. Students lead moral dilemma discussions.

With such concerted emphasis on the valuing ability, Alverno College is becoming expert in teaching values. Their major goal in liberal education is "to produce graduates who are morally responsible."[67] They have been implementing this goal in their curriculum since 1971.

Adult Level

We are now in the attic of our house called Moral Education in the Secular Domain. There is just one program I want to describe. It is a teacher education program. Sharon Oja and Norman Sprinthall have reviewed the dismal failure of thousands of in-service teacher education programs.[68] They decided to try the approach of psychological education based succintly on developmental theory. The developmental theories they chose were Loevinger's ego-development theory, Sullivan's conceptual development theory, and Kohlberg's moral-ethical theory.

Participants in a summer-school class at the University of Minnesota were in-service elementary and secondary school teachers. One of the general objectives of the program was "increased principled morality."[69] That is the reason for including this program as an example of values education. The entire program had three phases. The purpose of Phase I was to build interpersonal relationships. The purpose of Phase II was to learn skills of facilitative teaching and to learn cognitive-developmental theory. Phase I and II occurred at the summer workshop. The purpose of Phase III was to apply skills and theory in real classroom settings. Phase III, the practicum, occurred during the fall quarter as teachers returned to their classrooms. The teachers were supervised and supported during the practicum phase.

Each phase illustrated the action-reflection framework which has been mentioned before. Role-taking, practice in facilitative communication skills and group process skills, discussions, and behavioral contracting were some of the strategies used in Phase I and Phase II. The study of cognitive-developmental theory did contribute to increasing the teacher's Kohlbergian stages in principled morality. However, the authors are quick to point out that the total environment must be carefully planned based on developmental theory. Interpersonal relationships are important to personal growth. Competency in teaching skills is important to personal growth. Support during periods of disequilibrium in new learning is also important.

Conclusion

We have come a long way in our tour of the house of Moral Education in the Secular Domain. We have been in small rooms based solely on Kohlbergian theory of moral development. And we have been in larger rooms based on multiple theories. The small rooms had programs involving only Rokeach's instrumental moral values. The larger rooms had programs involving Rokeach's instrumental values from both the moral and competency categories. Certainly Rokeach's terminal values, both personal and social, are involved in these larger rooms as psychological maturity is encouraged. A learner is a whole person who is developing.

Chapter 5 Notes and References

1. John Westerhoff III and Gwen Kennedy Neville, *Generation to Generation* (Philadelphia: United Church Press, 1974), pp. 37–45.

2. John H. Peatling, *Religious Education in a Psychological Key* (Birmingham, Ala.: Religious Education Press, 1981), p. 135.

3. Louis E. Raths, Merrill Harmin, and Sidney B. Simon, *Values and Teaching* (Columbus, Ohio: Charles E. Merrill, 1966).

4. Sidney B. Simon, Leland W. Howe, and Howard Kirschenbaum, *Values Clarification* (New York: Hart Publishing Co., 1972).

5. Jack Canfield and Harold C. Wells, *100 Ways to Enhance Self-Concept in the Classroom* (Englewood Cliffs, N.J.: Prentice-Hall, Inc., 1976).

6. See James B. Macdonald, "A Look at the Kohlberg Curriculum Framework For Moral Education" in *Moral Development, Moral Education and Kohlberg*, ed. Brenda Munsey (Birmingham, Ala.: Religious Education Press, 1980).

7. James S. Clinefelter and Charles R. Knicker, "Does Values Clarification Go Far Enough?" in *Character Potential* 9(3) (November, 1980).

8. Mary M. Wilcox, *Developmental Journey* (Nashville: Abingdon, 1979).

9. Joseph Lukinsky, "Two Cheers for Value Confusion," *Religious Education* 75(6) (November-December, 1980).

10. John L. Harrison, "Values Clarification: An Appraisal," *Journal of Moral Education* 6(1) (October, 1976).

11. James S. Leming, "Curricular Effectiveness in Moral/Values Education," *Journal of Moral Education* 10(3) (May, 1981).

12. These centers are: 1. National Humanistic Education Center, Upper Jay, N.Y., 2. Institute for Humanistic Education of the New England Center, Amherst, 3. The Center for Humanistic Education, Amherst, Mass. 4. Values Associates, Amherst, Mass. and 5. Search, Minneapolis, Minn.

13. Joel Goodman, ed. *Turning Points: New Developments, New Directions in Values Clarification* (Saratoga Springs, N.Y.: Creative Resources Press, 1978).

14. Howard Kirschenbaum, "Values Clarification and Civil Liberties," *Moral Education Forum* 5(3) (Fall, 1980).

15. Mary M. Wilcox, *Developmental Journey*, pp. 210–212.

16. William Damon, ed. *Moral Development: New Directions for Child Development* (San Francisco: Jossey-Boss Inc., 1978). Also Norman A. Sprinthall and Ralph L. Mosher, *Values Development . . . As the Aim of Education* (Schenectady, N.Y.: Character Research Press, 1980).

17. Lisa Kuhmerker, ed. *Moral Education Forum* 4(1) (Spring, 1979).

18. Ibid. 5(1) (Spring, 1980).

19. Ibid. 6(1) (Spring, 1981).

20. Ibid.

21. Monica J. Taylor, ed., *The Journal of Moral Education* (Social Morality Council).

22. See Ralph L. Mosher, ed., *Moral Education: A First Generation of Research and Development* (New York: Praeger, 1980).

23. Linda Rosenzweig, "Kohlberg in the Classroom: Moral Education Models," in *Moral Development, Moral Education, and Kohlberg*, ed. Brenda Munsey (Birmingham, Ala.: Religious Education Press, 1980).

24. Lawrence Kohlberg, "Educating for a Just Society," in *Moral Development, Moral Education, and Kohlberg*, pp. 455–470.

25. Suzanne L, Krogh, "Moral Beginnings: The Just Community in Montessori Pre-Schools," *Journal of Moral Education* 11(1) (October, 1981).

26. Ibid., p. 45.

27. My acquaintance with Montessori methods is through Jerome Berryman's work with young children at the Institute of Religion at the Texas Medical Center in Houston. For readers who want more information I recommend a book of her lectures titled *The Absorbent Mind* (New York: Holt, Rinehart and Winston, 1967) (English translation) and a biography by E. M. Standing, *Maria Montessori: Her Life and Work* (New York: Mentor-Omega Books, 1957).

28. Lucie W. Barber and John H. Peatling, *Realistic Parenting* (St. Meinrad, Ind.: Abbey Press, 1980).

29. The program, *Realistic Parenting,* is built around the *Barber Scales of Self-Regard* which, in turn, are based on a Group Model of Personality. See John H. Peatling and David V. Tiedeman, *Career Development: Designing Self* (Muncie, Ind.: Accelerated Development, Inc., 1977).

30. The descriptions of Kohlberg's first three stages are taken from *Fairy Tales Revisited,* a teacher booklet put out in 1980 by the Values Education Project and Reading Centre of the Scarborough, Ontario Schools.

31. R. L. Selman and M. Lieberman, "An Evaluation of a Cognitive-Developmental Values Curriculum for Primary Grade Children," *Journal of Educational Psychology* 67(1975), pp. 712–716.

32. D. S. Biskin and K. Hoskisson, "An Experimental Test of the Effects of Structured Discussions of Moral Dilemmas Found in Children's Literature on Moral Reasoning," *Elementary School Journal* 77(1977), pp. 407–416.

33. Robert D. Enright, "A Classroom Discipline Model for Promoting Social Cognitive Development in Early Childhood," *Journal of Moral Education* 11(1) (October, 1981).

34. Friendship skills are based on Selman's (1976) theory on stages of interpersonal conceptions. More will be said about Selman's stages in chapter 8.

35. Social problem skills are based on Spivack and Shure, 1974.

36. Valerie Ostarch, "Cross-Age Teaching: Stimulus to Moral Development," *Moral Education Forum* 6(3) (Fall, 1981).

37. Psychological education, in the sense used here, is described in R. Mosher and N. Sprinthall, "Deliberate Psychological Education," *Counseling Psychologist* 2(4) (1973).

38. A description of Grimes doctoral dissertation work can be found in David E. Stuhr's chapter, "Moral Education With Chil-

dren," in *Value Development . . . As the Aim of Education*, pp. 41–52.

39. Gloria Jane Wallin, "Fostering Moral Development Through Creative Dramatics." *The Personnel and Guidance Journal* 58(9) (May, 1980).

40. The commercial materials were taken from *Developing Values.* Guidance Associates, 1976.

41. Robert D. Enright, "Promoting Interpersonal and Moral Growth in Elementary Schools," in *Value Development . . . As the Aim of Education*, pp. 27–40.

42. Paul J. Sullivan and Mary F. Dockstader, "Values Education and American Schools: Worlds in Collision?" in *Value Development . . . As the Aim of Education*, pp. 135–156.

43. Ibid., p. 147.

44. Paul J. Sullivan and Mary Dockstader Sullivan, "Establishing Moral Education Programs: A Priority for Guidance," *The Personnel and Guidance Journal* 58(9) (May, 1980).

45. Ralph L. Mosher and Norman A. Sprinthall, "Psychological Education in Secondary Schools," *American Psychologist*, 25 (1970).

46. Norman A. Sprinthall and Ralph L. Mosher, "John Dewey Revisited: A Framework for Developmental Education," in *Value Development . . . As the Aim of Education*, pp. 16–26.

47. Philip V. Cognetta and Norman A. Sprinthall, "Students as Teachers: Role Taking as a Means of Promoting Psychological and Ethical Development During Adolescence," in *Value Development . . . As the Aim of Education*, pp. 53–68.

48. Kohlberg, "Educating for a Just Society," *Moral Development, Moral Education, and Kohlberg*, pp. 455–470.

49. Ralph L. Mosher, "A Democratic High School: Damn It, Your Feet Are Always in the Water," *Value Development . . . As the Aim of Education*, pp. 69–116.

50. Linda Rosenzweig, "Kohlberg in the Classroom: Moral Education Models," *Moral Development, Moral Education, and Kohlberg*, pp. 359–380.

51. The entire Winter 1981 issue of *Moral Education Forum,* 6(4) is devoted to describing the Scarsdale Alternative School's *Just Community.*

52. Ibid., p. 9.

53. Ibid., p. 10.

54. Ibid., p. 18.

55. There are programs for personal growth at the University of Nebraska-Lincoln and at Azusa Pacific College and at other colleges. But the relationship to values education is nebulous.

56. John H. Whiteley, *Character Development in College Students* (Schenectady, N.Y.: Character Research Press, 1982), p. 82.

57. Ibid., p. 88.

58. Ibid., p. 107.

59. *Character Development in College Students* is Volume I in a planned three Volume series. Volume 2 is in press.

60. Whiteley, *Character Development in College Students,* p. 101.

61. Ibid., p. 102.

62. Marcia Mentkowski, "Creating a Mindset for Evaluating a Liberal Arts Curriculum Where Valuing is a Major Outcome," in *Evaluating Moral Development* (Schenectady, N.Y.: Character Research Press, 1980), p. 31.

63. Ibid., pp. 30–31. The other of the eight outcomes are: effective communication ability, analytical capability, problem solving ability, effective social interaction, effectiveness in individual/environment relationships, responsible involvement in the contemporary world, and aesthetic responsiveness.

64. Ibid., p. 32.

65. Ibid., p. 34.

66. Ibid., p. 35.

67. Ibid., p. 30.

68. Sharon N. Oja and Norman A. Sprinthall, "Psychological and Moral Development for Teachers: Can You Teach Old Dogs?" in *Value Development . . . As the Aim of Education.*

69. Ibid., p. 122.

CHAPTER 6

The Potential in Teaching
Values

We have spent the last two chapters looking at ways to teach values. Chapter 4 gave examples of how religious educators teach values. Chapter 5 gave examples of how secular educators teach values. Can we somehow pull all of this information together into a useful package? Can we begin to get a vision of what values education might be in the future of religious education? It is my purpose in this chapter to answer those two questions. It is particularly my purpose to portray a vision for the future.

I am going to organize this chapter into two main categories. The first category will be about what religious and secular educators have in common in teaching values. The second category will be about what religious and secular educators have *somewhat* in common. My hope is that my vision of what *can be* in religious education will be illuminated in the second category.

In Common

There are five areas where I see religious and secular educators in juxtaposition. Both groups of educators are in agreement.

1. *Values education is intentional.* Some people believe that values are caught rather than taught. However, these people are not educators. Religious and secular educators are deliberate, purposeful, and intentional in teaching values.

2. *Values education is an open-ended system.* The religious and secular educators we have inspected are not engaged in indoctrination. All have a healthy respect for the value of each and every learner. This is particularly true of Gillespie and Dykstra in the Individual Fulfillment School, and of Mosher and Sprinthall in psychological education. All values educators are future oriented. And all are interested in the learner's potential. Thus, values education must be open-ended. Even Kohlberg's six stages are open-ended in the sense that examples of stage six cannot be found.[1]

3. *Teachers are facilitators in values education.* If values education is not indoctrination, then teachers facilitate learning. We saw this image of the teacher in both Gillespie and Dykstra. It is true in moral education as well. Teachers present moral dilemmas. Then they let students seek answers for themselves. Teachers in a just community share power with students. Teachers cannot be authoritarians when such values as fairness and forgiveness are being taught.

4. *Teachers are arrangers of the learning environment.* This is most apparent in James Michael Lee's work. However, it is true for all the religious educators cited and is certainly true in every room we visited in the house called Moral Education in the Secular Domain. The environment is most arranged in just community schools and at Alverno College and in the Sierra Project.

5. *The importance of theory.* The theories to which religious educators attach importance are apt to be theological. Miller, Dykstra, and Gillespie espouse particular theologies. Wilcox, Lee, and Westerhoff are more eclectic about theology. But they do belong to cultural settings which imply a theological heritage. Lee comes out of the Roman Catholic heritage. Wilcox and Westerhoff belong to a liberal Protestant setting. Both Wilcox and Lee also take theory from psychologists.

The theories of importance to the secular values educators are usually psychological. Also, the psychological theorists tend to be developmental psychologists. At the present moment I am trying to indicate points in common. Religious and secular educators agree that in values education theory is important. The worthwhileness of theory is a cliche. However, we must not forget this worthwhileness anymore than we can forget intentionality, open-ended systems, and teachers as facilitators and arrangers of the learning environments. Let us celebrate agreements and, then, seek further.

The seeking further is where so many religious educators get themselves caught in a trap. They do not believe that they need to seek further. The Spirit will guide them.

I believe that God's Spirit should guide religious educators. When I go out to do a workshop or participate in a consultancy, I sincerely pray that God can work through me by her/his Spirit to bring about God's goals. However, I am only one finger or one toe of the body of Christ. I have to be responsible for my functioning. That means I must know as much as I can about the whole. As imperfect as I am, I must do my best. I cannot at a very practical level expect to be bailed out by the Spirit.

Thus, I take you into the next section on "Somewhat In Common" in the hope that together we, with our imperfections, can learn more about teaching values. I am guiding this tour so that I will be calling the shots.[2] I hope that you will see something that I haven't. We saw some remarkable things going on in values education in religious education. I think we saw some even more remarkable things in chapter 5.

Somewhat in Common

This will be a longer section because I see nine areas to be discussed. All areas are related to each other and to the five areas presented in the first section.

1. *The lists of values.* The list of values which are taught in the secular domain in moral education includes justice, fairness, cooperation, responsibility, good decision making, and other instrumental values. Religious educators would not omit these values. They would add faith, hope, and love, to the list. Moreover, Christian educators would specify the faith, hope, and love so that these values include the great commandments about loving God, one's

neighbor, and one's self. Loving God by implication involves terminal values. Loving one's self involves personal and competency values. Thus, while religious and secular educators' lists of values have much in common, religious educators have expanded lists of greater scope. In fact, religious values are a distinguishing factor between religious education and secular education. It is possible to teach history, mathematics, science, geography, and so forth, without teaching values. It is *not* possible to teach faith, hope, and love without teaching values. You can teach *about* religion without teaching values. But religious educators hope to teach religion as a living faith. They must teach values.

2. *The lists of strategies.* The lists of strategies in both the religious and secular domain include role playing, moral dilemma discussions, dramatizations, the use of filmstrips, movies, and other audio-visuals, values clarification exercises, cross-age teaching and counseling, interviewing, and diary keeping. Religious and secular educators have the list of strategies in common. The difference lies in the use made of all the strategies. I suspect that the more complicated strategies are used more often by the secular educators. I suspect that religious educators lack funds and time for the more complicated strategies. They should not lack knowledge, but perhaps they do.

3. *Devotion to a long-term process.* I have been inspired by the devotion of Mosher and Sprinthall and other moral educators in the secular domain to a long-term process.[3] Teachers attrition in schools has been heavy.[4] Yet the leaders keep trying. The just community takes at least two years to begin to pay off. Stage development in the smaller

rooms of our house applies to less than half of the kids, and then it represent only movement of a quarter stage on the average.[5] Despite continuous discouragement, the moral educators keep trying. Their annual conventions, their publications, and their personal commitment somehow keep them going. They will not give up on their mission.

I also see deep commitment to a mission among religious educators. They, too, will not give up. They, too, encounter continuous discouragement. They, too, encounter attrition on the part of volunteer Sunday School teachers. Volunteer Sunday School teachers want instant band-aids for their pupils.

The leaders in religious education keep going on a long-term process because they must—they are devoted to a religious way of living. My stance is that unless and until religious educators will admit the importance of values education, they will be missing the boat. I believe that our outstanding religious educators see values education as important. My concern is that many religious educators do not see values education as important.

Religious and secular educators are somewhat in agreement that values education is important as a long-term process. We need more who are so committed.

4. *The importance of teacher training.* Here is some agreement but not a great deal. Secular educators more and more *insist* upon teacher training. They have quite realistically faced the problem of Kohlbergian Stage 3 teachers teaching students who are at Stage 4. It is impossible. Teachers need training toward Stage 4 and personal growth toward Stage 5. I described just such a program in

chapter 5 at the attic level. Teachers need knowledge of developmental theory and need to be developing themselves.

I am sure that religious institutions intend to train their teachers, and some do. However, I think we can learn from secular moral educators about what kind of training is necessary. We need training in developmental theory. We need training in facilitative teaching skills. We need action and reflection. We need supervision in practicums. And we need to engage in personal growth.

5. *The importance of family.* Here, we have an edge on moral education in the secular domain. At least, religious education theoretically has the edge. Practitioners are convinced of the role of parents as primary religious educators of their children. Secular school teachers are only, within the past five years, beginning to explore ways to be partners with parents. The Grimes Room described in chapter 5 is an exception. The success of that effort in moral education is sure to be repeated as secular educators continue to explore in a long-term process.

When I say that religious educators have the edge, let me point out a caveat. Religious educators at the parish level, while convinced of the importance of parents, still, all too often, do not know what to do. I would speculate that there are four reasons why parishes do not know what to do:

1. Each parish is unique. The St. Swithins parish has problems X and Y. The Goodwill parish has problems A and B. A program to solve problems M and N applies to

neither. That is an oversimplification, to be sure. But the problems of parents and of training them differ from parish to parish.

2. Parishes want to be independent. This may be another way of saying that many parishes are suspicious of their denominational hierarchy. What can people in big-city offices know of the needs of rural parishes? Actually headquarters make it their business to know. Communications need improvement.

3. Volunteer religious educators are too often of the one-hour-a-week, Sunday School variety with little or no training. While there is no denying that some Sunday School teachers are exceedingly gifted in dealing with children, that does not necessarily translate into giftedness with the childrens' parents. Parishes need specially trained parent educators who are certified to train parents.[6]

4. Parishes lack access to institutions or centers where they can send candidates for training to become parent educators. Seminaries, colleges, and universities are only beginning to pay attention to family ministries. Only a few focus on preparing students to teach parents how to engage in values education with their children.

I have written that religious educators have the edge on moral educators on the importance of family. I have also outlined where we are in advance and where we can improve. However, I do not see any advantage in putting religious education in competition with secular moral education. Religious educators must learn from secular moral educators, and vice versa. If we could rally all the troops on the importance of family, we could add to the effectiveness of teaching values.

6. *The action-reflection model.* Perhaps this concept should have been placed in Section 1—In Common. I place it here in Somewhat in Common because I do not think that either secular educators or religious educators really appreciate the principle. The principle itself is simple enough—you get the learner to engage in an action and then reflect upon what has happened. This was John Dewey's approach, and it is sound.

I see the action-reflection approach with Gillespie and Dykstra. They do not want to hurry decisions. Nor do I. Nor do most religious educators with whom I am acquainted. Nonetheless, I suspect that many religious educators do not appreciate the strength of the action-reflection model. Values Clarification and Kohlbergians want to press for decisions. I suspect that many confirmation classes for young teenagers are pressure cookers for decisions and lack opportunities for adequate reflection.

7. *Community—the concept.* Both religious and secular educators appear to believe in the concept of community in values education. The differences crop up in the kind of community each aspires to and the intentionality about building such a community. Secular educators aspire to a just community as we have seen. The students learn democracy by living democratically. It is interesting how soon after the introduction of moral dilemmas discussions in classrooms the idea of a just community began in schools. And once the influence of the environment was recognized, secular educators attacked the problem and

began experimenting with the concept of a just community. Kohlberg, Mosher, and Fenton did not fool around. They deliberately changed the entire governance structure in their projects. Rules, hiring, firing, discipline were decided on the bases of each person, student or faculty, having one vote.

Religious educators aspire to a different kind of community, a community of faith, hope, and love. Yet we are much less specific about how we obtain such a community. Certainly one person—one vote will not do it. I believe that part of the difficulty is that Christians have lived with the concept of community since the first century and assume that every parish is a community. Every parish, unfortunately, is not a community of faith, hope, and love. Some parishes are communities of bigots, status seekers, and status preservers.

I believe that religious educators can take the concept of community as a necessary component (the environmental component) in values education and be much more specific about how to establish community in parishes, schools, colleges, or wherever Christians are gathered together. John Westerhoff would have us tell and retell the biblical story, pray together, worship together, serve and witness together. That is not specific enough for me. There is something missing. That something is contained in all the points I have discussed. I will try to draw out that something after we have looked at my last two points.

8. *Teaching the whole person.* Secular, moral educators are quite specific when they talk about the whole person as best as they can understand, psychologically, what a whole person is. Their theories include Piaget (cognition), Kohlberg

(moral judgment), Loevinger (ego-development), Selman (interpersonal development), Dupont (emotional development), and others.[7] John Dewey originated in our century the concept of teaching the whole person. He was limited because he did not have the knowledge of developmental theories which we have today. Secular educators have grabbed on to these theories. Religious educators have been noticeably slower. I, for one, have been a slow religious educator. Nonetheless, I am now convinced that we must have a clearer understanding of the whole person (the learner). I am now convinced that developmental theories are the way to go.

There is a religious educator who is on her way in exploring teaching the whole learner. That is Mary Wilcox. She diagrams the whole learner in a pie diagram. She is still mostly concerned with the cognitive piece of the pie. But, she is wrestling with religious education as teaching the whole person. Iris Cully is another religious educator concerned with multiple developmental theories. Barber and Peatling are interested in the whole person who is the learner. Religious educators no longer ignore psychological theories. Let us hope that the openness continues.

9. *Teaching to the developmental level.* This last point is, of course, closely associated with point 8 and, for that matter, with all other points. In fact, I consider this point the most important of all (given the other points). When educators have a better understanding of their learners, they can do a better educational job. That sounds so simple. Yet educators have paid little attention to common sense. We have gone for too many years on the assumption that adults know what is right. Therefore, teachers were the au-

thorities. Knowledge (the adults' knowledge) was poured into children's minds. Yet the pouring in does not work.

Now we have access to what may in the future be labeled wisdom. The developmental levels provided by empirical research in the past few decades let us take a radically different approach to education. Teach to developmental level. Children are not miniature adults and, furthermore, they are quite different from adults. Unless educators understand the differences, educational efforts are in trouble. As a matter of fact, educational efforts will fail as they have in the past.

Ronald Goldman was an early proponent of religious educators paying attention to developmental level.[8] John Peatling followed up on Goldman's work. So did Mary Wilcox, Lucie Barber, Iris Cully, James Fowler, John Elias, Larry Loconsy, and others in religious education.[9]

In practical terms, teaching to developmental level means a realistic approach. If the learner is at Stage 1, the learner is stimulated only to Stage 2. If the learner is at Stage 2, the learner is stimulated only to Stage 3, etc. Learners are realistically stimulated to only one further stage. This is common sense and so simple we failed to see the realism and the practicality.

Now I believe that we can no longer ignore the evidence in religious education. We cannot bury our heads in the sand while exciting progress is being made in developmental theory. We must teach to developmental level. I am not saying that all our problems will be solved. Knowledge inflates exponentially at an alarming rate. As faithful Christians our responsibility is to keep abreast of new knowledge. "Happy are they who hunger and thirst after righteousness, for they shall be filled" (Matthew 5:6).

A Vision for Teaching Values in Religious Education

The future of religious education must be addressed in the present. Since religious education is intentional and deliberate, goals must be set. What are the values to be taught? I will stick with faith, hope, and love for the time being. Since religious education is open ended, the learners must eventually guide their own learning and be responsible for themselves. It is the learners who choose what values they will own. Thus, teachers must be facilitators. Teachers must be master arrangers of the environment so that learners are challenged toward new levels of thought and feeling.

However, there is background work to be done. The community life in the parish needs to be upgraded. This means that adults in the parish must understand the children as developing persons, not as miniature adults. A good dose of developmental theory would be helpful. Sermons on developmental theory might be a way to go. Adult classes is another way. Booklets, newsletters, or audio-visuals are other ways. Solid teacher training and parent training are essential in improving community and in educating the children and the adult teachers and parents. Whatever the efforts in your parish, I would suggest sharing the efforts with all members so that all can become involved in teaching faith, hope, and love.

There must be devotion to a long-term process. The action-reflection model is important in values education. Action-reflection takes time; sometimes, a great deal of time. However, it is worth it in a long-term process because it promotes learners really owning the values they choose. Such learning requires teachers who are facilitator-guides.

Now we come to the teacher-learner interaction moment. The teacher must be aware that she/he is teaching the whole person—not just the cognitive learner, the social skills learner, the emotional learner or the action learner. The best way to teach the whole learner is for the teacher to understand multiple developmental theories and then teach to developmental level.

All fourteen points that have been mentioned in this chapter are important and interrelated. I believe that the king pin for all fourteen points lies in the respect for and importance of each and every person as God's daughter or son. Knowledge of developmental theories will assist us in respecting and valuing all persons. Thus, the entire next section of this book will be devoted to developmental theory.

Chapter 6 Notes and References

1. It might be well to note that Kohlberg has said "I now believe that the concepts guiding moral education must be partly indoctrinative." See his chapter, "Revisions in the Theory and Practice of Moral Development" in *Moral Development: New Directions for Child Development* (San Francisco, Jossey-Bass Inc., No. 2, 1978). See also Kohlberg's chapter, "Educating for a Just Society: An Updated and Revised Statement," in *Moral Development, Moral Education, and Kohlberg*, ed. Brenda Munsey (Birmingham, Ala.: Religious Education Press, 1980). To my knowledge the other secular, moral educators have not claimed indoctrination, particularly not Mosher & Sprinthall. They persist in their efforts for an open-ended system. See Mosher's latest book *Moral Education: A First Generation of Research and Development* (New York: Praeger, 1980).

2. In fairness to you the reader, I wish to explain how I chose the six contemporary religious educators found in chapter 4.

Very simply, they were the only ones to my knowledge who have written anything directly about how they would teach values. Iris Cully does have a discussion about how others teach values. See *Christian Child Development* (San Francisco: Harper & Row, 1979), pp. 88–102.

3. See *Moral Education: A First Generation of Research and Development.* Also *Values Development . . . As the Aim of Education,* ed. Norman A. Sprinthall and Ralph L. Mosher (Schenectady, N.Y.: Character Research Press, 1978); also *Evaluating Moral Development,* ed. Kuhmerker, Mentkowski, and Erickson (Schenectady, N.Y.: Character Research Press, 1980).

4. Ibid., p. 215.

5. Ibid., p. 214.

6. The author was a member of a team, along with Doris Blazer, Edgar Hartley, John Peatling, and John Westerhoff, who presented an extensive proposal for a Parent Educationl Program at the Kanuga retreat center. Kanuga is an Episcopalian center in North Carolina. The proposal envisioned a two-year program leading to certification of trainees as parent educators.

7. *Values Development . . . As the Aim of Education,* chap. 2, "John Dewey Revisited: A Framework for Developmental Education."

8. See these two books by Goldman: *Religious Thinking from Childhood to Adolescence,* and *Readiness for Religion* (London: Routledge and Kegan Paul, 1964 and 1965 respectively).

9. Wilcox's, Barber's and Cully's work have already been referenced. James W. Fowler, *Stages of Faith* (San Francisco: Harper & Row, 1981). John L. Elias, *Psychology and Religious Education* (Betheleham, Pa: Catechetic Communications, 1975), and Lawrence Losoncy, *Religious Education and the Life Cycle* (Same publisher, 1977).

Don't Forget Development

CHAPTER 7

Affective and Cognitive Theories

As we have seen in Section II, the learner is a whole. Furthermore, a way to learn about and understand a whole person (the learner) is to study multiple developmental theories. Studying only one developmental theory is not enough. That is lop-sided understanding. Studying only two developmental theories is an improvement but still not enough. Fortunately, we have access to multiple theories today which have believable empirical bases.

I propose in this section to introduce you to nine developmental theories. My criteria for choosing the nine are twofold. First, I believe that these theories are new to you. Second, if the theories are not entirely new to you, I believe I can perhaps give you a glimpse of newness that you may have so far missed. For example, did you know that Piaget evolved a theory of affective development?

Thus, I will not be describing the theories of Piaget on cognition, or Kohlberg, Erikson, Allport, Skinner, or even

Fowler. You can read about these theorists elsewhere if you are not acquainted with them. In fact, if you are not acquainted with these theories I strongly recommend that you become contemporary in matters of general knowledge. My goal is to bring you closer to the razor's edge.

I have divided the section into four chapters. Affectivity and cognition will be addressed in this chapter. Interpersonal theories of development will be addressed in chapter 8. Chapter 9 will cap off the whole person approach with theories on ego-development and self-actualization.

The nine theories will be introduced as strands in a Golden Braid. In chapter 10, I will make the attempt to deal with the Golden Braid as a whole (the whole learner).

The focus of this whole section is on understanding the learner. Throughout these chapters, there is another focus, namely illustrations of the fourteen points elucidated in chapter 6 which describe my vision of values in religious education. Of course, an understanding of the learner through attention to developmental theories encompasses the points about teaching the whole learner and teaching to developmental level. However, we must not forget community, the action-reflection model, the importance of family, the importance of teacher (parent) training, devotion to a long-term process, lists of values, lists of strategies, the importance of theory, and teachers as intentional in an open-ended process, as facilitative guides and arrangers of the environment.

Introduction to Affectivity and Cognition

You may wonder that I put the affective and cognitive strands together in one chapter. I do so quite purposively.

68203

I am aware that psychologists have diochotomized these two strands. For example, R. B. Zajonc[1] working from his own research and the research of others believes that affective reactions as opposed to cognitive reactions are primary (come first), are basic, inescapable, irrevocable, implicate the self, are difficult to verbalize, do not depend on cognitions, and can be separated from content. Zajonc further believes that stimuli are processed separately by the two systems, affective and cognitive, as does Rogers.[2] Another psychologist, Julian Jaynes,[3] has written a lengthy book wherein he uses evidence from not only psychology but also from history, literature, archeology, and anthropology. He describes early man as a creature ruled by the right hemisphere of the brain which he would appear to equate with the affective system.[4] Humans in the B.C. centuries were driven by the voices of their gods. Jaynes tends to equate religion with the voices and completes his book by suggesting that present-day man has no further use for religion because the left hemisphere is increasingly taking over, which is for him a cognitive system. I object to his either right-hemisphere or left-hemisphere approach. That is too simplistic and premature.

From an entirely different source come yet more arguments for the primacy of the affective. This time it is the religious educator, Westerhoff.[5] He addresses himself directly to values. While Westerhoff is careful to say that both cognitive and affective systems are important in religious education, he says that the affective is primary. He does not directly talk about the right and left hemisphere of the brain. Instead, he talks about "a responsive-intuitive mode of thinking and . . . an active-intellectual mode of thinking."[6] The responsive-intuitive mode is affective, while the active-intellectual mode is cognitive. "Our values emerge, I contend, from feelings rather than through reasoning."[7] They emerge from the responsive-intuitive mode.

Lest you think at this point that I have stacked my cards for the affective group let me give you some arguments of a different nature. Richard Lazarus has been a leader in cognitive psychology for more than two decades. He recently took Zajonc to task for misinterpreting cognition as only information processing.[8] "Information processing as an exclusive model of cognition is insufficiently concerned with the person as a source of meaning."[9] Humans must make meaning if they are to survive in their environment. Every stimulus must be "appraised" for its threat or non-threat potential. "The cognitive activity in appraisal does not imply anything about deliberate reflection, rationality, or awareness."[10] Appraisal "inheres in the cognitive structures and commitments developed over a lifetime."[11] These "determine the personal and hence emotional significance of any person-environment encounter."[12] Thus from this broader understanding of the cognitive, Lazarus rejects the primacy of the affective. It is the other way around.

Lazarus' broader interpretation of the cognitive (as making meaning) is a generalization which transforms cognitions from only information processing or the rational thought definitions to a grander definition.

I believe Piaget went one step further on this idea of transformation. Lazarus transformed the meaning of cognition by generalizing the definition of cognition to a more inclusive definition. Piaget transformed the distinction between the affective and the cognitive into a whole by proclaiming that affective and cognitive are flip sides of the same coin. "Affective states that have no cognitive elements are never seen, nor are behaviors found that are wholly cognitive."[13]

Many of you have not yet read the Piaget book called *Intelligence and Affectivity*.[14] It is a slim volume published in English in this country in 1981. Most of us think of Piaget as a cognitivist. Actually he had a good deal to say about affect. He made the point that raising the question about affective and cognitive as separate systems was an *absurd* question.[15] For example, let me take a Zajonc example and play back a Piagetian response and a Lazarus response.

Zajonc: The rabbit hears a swish in the grass. He dashes for safety without waiting to analyze, rationally, the snake's fangs. The rabbit acted on a solely emotional basis.

Piagetian and Lazarus: The rabbit hears a swish in the grass. He dashes to safety. He has been trained by mother rabbit to react that way to any swish in the grass. To Lazarus this is a cognitive (trained) response. To Piaget it hardly matters whether it is affective or cognitive because the response is so instantaneous. It is an absurd question to raise.

Thus, I approach this chapter with the premise that affectivity and cognition can be transformed into one braid in a Golden Braid of nine theories.[16] Let us look at the two strands, affect and cognition, as one. I have found a Moebius strip useful in describing what I mean by transformation. Take a strip of paper two inches wide and 8 inches long. Draw lines down the middle length of each side. Label the line on one side "affective." Label the line on the other side "cognitive"—a seeming dichotomy. Now hold the strip out, twist one of the ends 180° and then tape the ends together. Do you see that whereas you began with two lines you now have one continuous line? A seeming dichotomy has been transformed.

Let us approach this chapter with a single line in mind. I will approach affective and cognitive developmental theories separately. However, my intention is a Golden Braid. We are approaching the *whole* learner, not just her/his intelligence or feelings.

Affective Development

Most discussions about affective development in psychology texts are about emotional development. They describe when certain emotions are evident in the infant and young child. Emotion denotes a strong feeling. Affectivity includes emotions, but it also includes all feelings in the sense that cognitivity includes all thinkings.

Dupont

Henry Dupont is presently working on a structural theory of affective development.[17] Dupont is grounded in Piaget. Table I outlines Dupont's stages in affective development plus indicating the themes and objects related to each stage.

Stage 1 is the infant's affectivity. Stage 2 is the structure of the preschooler's affectivity. Stage 3 is the stage elementary children can attain but some do not and are frozen, as it were, at stage 2.

Stage 4 describes the structure possible for mature adolescents and adults. Dupont has some empirical data in

Table I. Affective Development: A Piagetian Model Stages, Themes, and Objects

Stages	Themes and Objects	
1. Egocentric-Impersonal	(E)	Tension-relaxation and the self's actions.
2. Heteronomous	(H)	Getting and receiving, or being ignored or deprived by parents. Also being granted or denied opportunities by significant adults.
3. Interpersonal	(I)	Receiving or being denied affection, approval, acceptance, recognition from peers.
4. Personal-Autonomous	(P)	Success or failure to realize personal ideals, goals, and values.

support of these four stages in affective development. However, his work continues and his first book is in the process of being written. Watch for more from Dupont on affective development.

Piaget

Jean Piaget's slim volume, *Intelligence and Affectivity: Their Relationship During Child Development*,[18] was published in this country a few months after his death. The volume is only seventy-four pages long. Nonetheless, the volume is helpful in bringing together in one place Piaget's thoughts on affectivity.

At the outset it must be understood that Piaget considered affectivity the flip side of cognitivity. He objected

TABLE II.   STAGES OF INTELLECTUAL AND AFFECTIVE
DEVELOPMENT

A. Sensorimotor intelligence	Intra-individual feelings
I. *Hereditary organizations*	*Hereditary organizations*
These include reflexes and in-stincts present at birth.	These include instinctual drives and all other in-born affective reactions.
II. *First acquired schemes*	*First acquired feelings*
These include the first habits and differentiated percep-tions. They appear before the sensorimotor intelligence, properly so-called.	These are joys, sorrows, pleasantness, and un-pleasantness linked to perceptions as well as dif-ferentiated feelings of contentment and disap-pointment linked to action.
III. *Sensorimotor intelligence*	*Affects regulating intentional behavior*
This includes the structures ac-quired from six or eight months up to the acquisition of language in the second year.	These regulations include feelings linked to the ac-tivation and retardation of action along with ter-mination reactions such as feelings of success or failure.
B. Verbal intelligence	Interpersonal feelings
IV. *Preoperational representations*	*Intuitive affects*
Here action begins to be inter-nalized. Although this allows thought, such thought is not yet reversible.	These include elementary interpersonal feelings and the beginnings of moral feelings.

V. *Concrete operations*

This stage lasts from approximately 7 or 8 until 10 or 11 years of age. It is marked by the acquisition of elementary operations of classes and relations. Formal thought is still not possible.

Normative affects

This stage is characterized by the appearance of autonomous moral feelings with intervention of the will. What is just and what is unjust no longer depend on obedience to a rule.

VI. *Formal operations*

This stage begins around 11 or 12 years, but it is not completely realized until 14 or 15. It is characterized by thought employing the logic of propositions freed from their content.

Idealistic feelings

In this stage feelings for other people are overlaid by feelings for collective ideals. Parallel to this is the elaboration of the personality where the individual assigns himself a role and goals in social life.

strenuously to separating the two domains. Feelings, furthermore, can hasten or impede the structuring of cognitions, but they cannot change cognitive structure. In this sense, affectivity energizes cognition.

The relationship between intelligence and affectivity is functional. Affectivity is the energy upon which intelligence depends.

Piaget's stages of cognitive development are constructions, one building upon a preceding stage and reconstructing it. He understood affective stages in much the same way. Table II is Piaget's representation of parallel cognitive and affective stages of development.[19]

The division of intellectual stages into Sensorimotor and Verbal Intelligence may be unfamiliar. Nonetheless, it was necessary in order to relate cognitive stages to affective stages. Before language, the baby has intra-individual feelings. Thereafter, feelings are systemitized based on experiences with other people. The acquisition of language moves the child from nonsocial to social behavior. With social behavior come moral feelings, autonomous moral feelings, will, collective ideals, and individual goals.

For the purpose of this book, it may be helpful to take a closer look at Piaget's thinking about values.

Peculiar to stage 3 is the emergence of a value system. An object or a person has value vis-à-vis a child's action. From these primordial beginnings of valuing come subsequent feelings in stages 4, 5, and 6. As social life advances in stage 4, transformations occur in the domain of feelings analogous to the development of intellectual structures. Moral feelings begin their development. Rules are valued. Norms are recognized.

Development of valuing continues into stage 5. Autonomous moral feelings emerge. Rules can be modified. Piaget introduces the will at this stage as a decentration of values: "It consists of subordinating a given situation to a permanent scale of values."[20]

A new dimension of feelings develops in stage 6. Values flower as the person can feel about objects, other people, *and* ideas. We label the feelings about ideas as idealistic feelings. With idealistic feelings comes a valuing of self vis-à-vis society. Personality is established.

In conclusion Piaget makes a distinction between behaviors related to objects and behaviors related to people. "Both have structural or cognitive and energetic or affective aspects. In behaviors related to objects the structural aspects are the various empirical and logicomathematical knowledge structures while the energetic aspects are the interests, efforts, and intra-individual feelings that regulate behavior."[21] Thus with cognitivity and affectivity, you cannot have one without the other. The two strands are already woven together.

Cognitive Development

The work of Ronald Goldman in religious thinking is well known. He found the Piagetian stages of preoperational, concrete, and abstract thinking in his interviewees in England. He renamed these stages: prereligious, subreligious, and religious thinking.

Peatling

On beyond Goldman is John H. Peatling and his instrument, *Thinking About the Bible*.[22] Over ten years of experience with this instrument have accumulated. Literally thousands of subjects have responded: children, adolescents, and adults in this country, the United Kingdom, and Finland. Peatling's Very Concrete and Concrete Scales and Abstract and Very Abstract Scales show changes over age and grade levels.

Peatling has found empirical evidence for four plateaus in his data from children and adolescents.[23] Grade 4 students exhibit preplateau #1 where intuitive thinking is strong although concrete thinking is also exhibited. Plateau #1, Firmly Concrete, is exhibited from 4th grade through 7th grade depending on the social milieu (denomination). Inter-Plateau #1–2 exhibits further dropping away of intuitive thinking and the beginning decrease of concrete thinking. This is a transition period and extends from grades 6–8, again depending on social milieu.

Plateau #2 exhibits the first increase in a preference for abstract thinking. Late concrete thinking, however, is still dominant. Students from grades 6 through 12 appear to belong at Plateau #2. Social milieu appears to determine where in that grade range a particular denomination will fall.

Plateau #3 begins at grade 8 and is early abstract thinking which certainly has implications for educators.

It is not until grades 10, 11, and 12 (depending on social milieu) that abstract thinking is firmly entrenched. Subsamples included Episcopalians, Roman Catholics, Finnish students, and Missouri Synod Lutherans. The pattern of development is similar across these social milieux. Abstract thinking is a potential for all youth. But some denominations appear to delay abstract thinking longer than other denominations. A judgment is not implied here. It may be to the best advantage to the Lutherans not to encourage abstract thinking. The goals of the institution are at stake.

Do adults continue to develop cognitively? Peatling has found two more cognitive plateaus in a select sample of adults.[24] Abstract thinking increases after a peculiar decline in the 20s to a plateau in the 30s and another plateau in the 40s. More research is indicated. However, it is clear that educators should not make the mistake that cognitive development ends upon graduation from high school. It does not.

Perry

Cognitive development beyond adolescence has been studied by W. B. Perry.[25] Perry postulates positions for adolescents and adults on a progression starting with early abstract thinking. Positions 3 and 4 are Multiplicity. Then comes a transition crisis (Peating's decline in the 20s?) for Position 5, Relativism. Position 6, Commitment in Relativism, occurs when cognitive structures are transformed. Murphy and Gilligan have found empirical support for Perry's system.[26] Their longitudinal data followed nineteen-year-olds until they were twenty-seven.

They found a shift from logical thinking through transformations which recognize "the paradoxial interdependance of self and society, which then overrides the false simplicity of formal reason and replaces it with a more encompassing form of judgment."[27] They quote Piaget thusly, "Reason which expresses the highest form of equilibrium reunites intelligence and affectivity."

One final part of the strand, cognitive development, involves current work by Fisher et al.[28] These cognitive developmentalists are working on beyond Piaget. Their goals are 1) to expand the scope of theory and research, 2) to look for better methodologies, and 3) to integrate the effects of the environment more directly into cognitive-developmental theory. Many of their findings suggest that the emotional lives of children are intimately connected with their cognitive development and their social environment.

Summary

One's level of cognitive thinking about things religious (the Bible) can be readily assessed. Cognitive development does not stop in the teenage years; it continues into adulthood. Cognitive development is intimately related to emotional development in the social environment.

Teaching the Value of Faith

"Faith cannot be taught by any method of instruction; we can only teach religion."[29] Westerhoff goes on to say, "No matter what the rhetoric of our purpose, the school-instructional paradigm, modeled after modern psychology and pedagogy, leads us to focus on religion rather than faith. If for no other reason than this, the school-instructional paradigm needs to be questioned."[30] The school-instructional paradigm has been questioned. Modern psychologists and pedagogues in moral education have shown us new ways to teach values. Perhaps, after all, faith can be taught. But we must pay attention to the development of the whole learner in a long-term process.

In order to illustrate what I mean, I am going to describe a lesson at two age levels, preschool and late adolescence. We have discussed only affective and cognitive development so far. Thus the descriptions will be only partial. I have defined faith elsewhere as, "Trust in a God creator and the self-confidence to accept God's grace."[31]

Preschool Level

When a religious educator takes a developmental approach, there are background steps to be taken before any lesson planning can take place. What is the preschool learner's developmental level? We need to know this in order to *teach to developmental level.* The normal preschool child would most likely be at Dupont's Stage 2, Heteronomous. This stage has to do with the child's relationship to parents. Thus, the *importance of family* is called into prominence.

To proceed in the affective realm, Piaget says the preschooler is at his Stage 4, Intuitive affects which include the beginnings of interpersonal feelings and the start of morality.

Also, we have some help from Piaget in the cognitive realm. Preschoolers are preoperational. They think intuitively. They do not yet think in any manner of rationality as appreciated by older children or adults. Peatling and Perry cannot help us in understanding preschoolers because they did not attend to the formative years in cognition. They will be more helpful in the late adolescent example.

My previous work on values training in the religious education of preschoolers is pertinent here. My quest has been to *train parents* to understand development, to be able to assess level of development so that they can *teach to developmental level.* My conclusions then as now are to *understand the whole learner.* What cognitive and affective appreciation of faith can we teach a preschooler at her/his developmental level?

I cannot repeat here all that I have written elsewhere on teaching faith to preschool children. One of the educational objectives I have proposed which parents can teach their young children is the appreciation of nature and the laws of nature. Nature is God's handiwork. Small children so new to our world are easily awed by the beauties they see about them. Parents can encourage such awe and wonder, gradually linking the beauty with its creation by God. A single lesson, then, can be as simple as a parent saying, "What a beautiful sunset. Let us thank God for giving it to us."

There is more to that simple lesson than is immediately apparent. The parent has *arranged the environment* in the sense that the child sees a beautiful sunset. This may mean a trip to the country on an appropriate evening. The lesson is *open-ended* because the *facilitator* parent is not forcing appreciation on the child. One exposure to God's beauty probably will not result in much learning. This lesson is only a small part of a *long-term process.* Many, many such lessons must accumulate in the experience of the child in order to reinforce a true appreciation of nature as God's gift.

Late Adolescent Level

The jump to senior high from preschool is deliberate. The two developmental levels are drastically different. The contrast will heighten awareness of what it means to *teach to developmental level.*

In the affective domain we have jumped from Dupont's Egocentric-Impersonal Stage to an Interpersonal Stage or more probably a Personal-Autonomous Stage in feelings. It seems to me that the teacher (or parent) should be aware of the developmental differences between these two stages. The Interpersonal Stage is tied affectively to peers. The Personal-Autonomous Stage is tied to individual values. The teacher must know the differences for each and every learner.

Piaget, on the other hand, describes this stage, linked with abstract thinking, to collective ideals. He follows out the autonomy focus with the learner assigning to self roles and goals in social life.

What have we on cognition? Peatling tells us that late adolescents prefer abstract thinking. This means that they can "appreciate metaphors, analogies, and allegories."[32] Formal religious education must begin; religious education seems childish if it is continued in the manner fed to children.[33] The cognitive development of 10th, 11th, and 12th graders demands an entirely new approach. They are new people on the developmental journey. Heretofore, they have not been sufficiently challenged by religious education.[34]

Perry adds a little bit more about early abstract thinking. His talk about Positions translates into Stages. The label is Multiplicity for late adolescence. This must be turned into Relativism and finally Commitment in Relativism at a most mature level. For our present purposes in understanding *the whole learner,* we must be content with Multiplicity for the late adolescent. The late adolescent understands a multiplicity of alternatives for solving value questions. He is probably not yet, but almost ready for Relativism.

One aspect of working at this late adolescent level is the abundance of assessment tools. In determining cognitive level which can help religious educators teach *to developmental level* there is Peatling's *Thinking About the Bible,* and Rest's *Defining Issues.* And there are more tests being developed.[35]

A way to *understand the whole learner* is to assess developmental level. I believe that assessment must be built into religious education. We have instruments available. Why not use them? These instruments can help in *teaching to developmental level.*

Once we have determined that the learner thinks abstractly about a multiplicity of alternatives and feels idealistically about autonomous roles and goals in social life, what can the religious educator teach about faith? The challenge is enormous. The opportunities are without number, therefore I will single out one example as a suggestion for a developmental approach. This will not be a lesson plan in the strict sense. It will be a general plan for a weekend retreat.[36]

Day One. The youth arrive midmorning and are engaged in exercises of getting to know each other. The purpose here, of course, is the beginning of building a sense of *community* so important to any retreat experience. In the afternoon the youth view a movie which is stopped before resolutions to problems are achieved. This could be a movie about the life of Albert Schweitzer, Martin Luther King, Gandhi, or C. S. Lewis' *Tales of Narnia.* No matter what the portion of the movie, it would have to be a stimulus for Christian moral discussion following its presentation. After discussion, the assignment for the retreat is given. The youth, in small groups, are to dramatize problem resolutions which they will video tape for presentation on day two. The rest of day one's afternoon is devoted to acquainting the youth with the technical equipment for video taping.

Day Two. The morning is devoted to groups writing their scripts, assigning actors, and finally taping their problem solutions. The solutions of each small group are played back to the whole group. This is followed by discussion and reflection. The *action-reflection* model is put to use. The teacher is a *facilitator* in an *open-ended* system. The *environment has been arranged* to stimulate these abstract thinkers to think about their faith and to deal with their idealistic values.

Of course the example of a retreat for late adolescents is an example of religious education for the *whole learner.* It illustrates the affective and cognitive strands. It also illustrates much more. Certainly, the interpersonal strand is potent in any retreat situation. Thus, we move on in chapter 8 to interpersonal theories.

Chapter 7 Notes and References

1. R. B. Zajonc, "Feeling and Thinking: Preferences Need No Inferences," *American Psychologist* 35(2) (February, 1980).

2. T. B. Rogers, "Models of Man: The Beauty and/or the Beast," *Personality and Social Psychology Bulletin* 6(4) (1980).

3. Julian Jaynes, *The Origin of Consciousness in the Breakdown of the Bicameral Mind* (Boston: Houghton Mifflin, 1976).

4. Another religious educator who believes that the division into right and left lobes is premature is Andrew D. Thompson. See his chapter, "Empirical Research and Religious Experience," in *Aesthetic Dimensions of Religious Education,* ed. Gloria Durka and Joanmarie Smith (New York: Paulist Press, 1979).

5. John Westerhoff III, "Values for Today's Children," *Religious Education* 75(3) (May–June, 1980).

6. Ibid., p. 252.

7. Ibid., p. 253.

8. Richard S. Lazarus, "Thoughts on the Relations Between Emotion and Cognition," *American Psychologist* 37(9) (September, 1982).

9. Ibid., p. 1020.

10. Ibid., p. 1022.

11. Ibid.

12. Ibid.

13. Jean Piaget, *Intelligence and Affectivity: Their Relationship During Child Development* (Palo Alto, Calif.: Annual Reviews, Inc., 1981).

14. Ibid., p. 5.

15. Ibid., pp. 1–74.

16. The ideas of a Golden Braid and a Moebius strip were taken from Douglas R. Hofstadter, *Gödel, Escher, and Bach: An Eternal Golden Braid* (New York: Vintage Books, 1980).

17. Henry Dupont, "Affective Development: A Piagetian Model (unpublished manuscript, 1978).

18. Piaget, *Intelligence and Affectivity.*

19. Ibid., p. 14.

20. Ibid., p. 69.

21. Ibid., p. 74.

22. John H. Peatling, "Cognitive Development and Religion," *Character Potential: A Record of Research* 8(2) (August, 1977).

23. John H. Peatling, "Cognitive Development in Grades Four Through Twelve: The Incidence of Concrete and Abstract Religious Thinking in American Children, *Character Potential: A Record of Research* 7(1) (October, 1974).

24. Ibid.

25. W. B. Perry *Forms of Intellectual and Ethical Development in the College Years* (New York: Holt, Rinehart and Winston, 1968).

26. Carol Gilligan and John Michael Murphy, "Development from Adolescence to Adulthood: The Philosopher and the Dilemma of the Fact," in *New Directions for Child Development: Intellectual Development Beyond Childhood*, ed. Deanna Kuhn (San Francisco: Jossey Bass Publishers, 1979).

27. Ibid.

28. Kurt W. Fischer et al., *New Directions for Child Development: Cognitive Development* (San Francisco: Jossey Bass Publishers, 1981).

29. John H. Westerhoff III, *Will Our Children Have Faith?* (New York: Seabury Press, 1976), p. 23.

30. Ibid.

31. Lucie W. Barber *The Religious Education of Preschool Children* (Birmingham, Ala.: Religious Education Press, 1981), p. 25.

32. John H. Peatling, "Religious Thinking in Adolescence," in *Knowing and Helping Youth,*ed. G. Temp Sparkman (Nashville: Broadman Press, 1977), p. 69.

33. Ronald Goldman, *Readiness for Religion* (London: Routledge and Kegan Paul, 1965).

34. A. Roger Gobbel, "Christian Education with Adolescents: An Invitation to Thinking," *The Living Light* 17(2), 1980.

35. *Evaluating Moral Development: And Evaluating Educational Programs That Have a Value Dimension*, ed. Lisa Kuhmerker, Marcia Mentkowski, and V. Lois Erickson (Schenectady, N.Y.: Char-

acter Research Press, 1980) gives information about some 15 instruments. Also see James R. Rest, *Development in Judging Moral Issues* (University of Minnesota Press, 1979), for a complete description of the *Defining Issues Test.*

36. My description of a weekend retreat is an adaptation of a Values and Video Day. See James S. Clinefelter and Charles R. Knicker, "Does Values Clarification Go Far Enough?" *Character Potential: A Record of Research* 9(3) (November, 1980), pp. 155–165.

CHAPTER 8

The Interpersonal Strands

The whole learner is more than a thinking and feeling person. The whole learner must relate to other people. Fortunately, development in interpersonal skills has been studied. We will look at the work of Robert Selman on social perspective taking, John Peatling on the development of moral judgment, and David Tiedeman on career decision making. Social perspective taking involves the skill of being able to understand others' perspectives. Moral judgment involves judging good and bad for self and others. Career decision making involves responsibility in decision making for making a career beneficial to self and others.

Social Perspective Taking

Robert Selman

Members of the Harvard-Judge Baker Social Reasoning

Project have been studying social cognition in children since 1973 under the directorship of Robert Selman.[1] Their goal has been to understand how children learn to take the perspective of others as they develop from childhood to adolescence. Through intensive interviews with children they found five stages which are developmental. Table III summarizes the stages as published in 1976.[2]

There is a wealth of information in Table III which may be helpful to religious educators. For example, it is useless to expect a preschooler to understand why a friend is unhappy from the friend's point of view. A seven-year-old may partially understand the friend's distress. Nine-year-old children take turns and understand their friend's feelings one at a time. It is not until the teenage years that social perspective taking matures.

While it is entirely possible to teach young children sympathetic behaviors, they can only gradually understand the perspective of others as they develop. The Christian value system, love, must be taught step by step with the stages of social perspective taking in mind. The same would be true for teaching forgiveness and mercy and also resolution of conflicts.

Selman and his colleagues have pushed further in their studies of social cognition. They have looked for stages in three categories: individual, friendship, and peer group. Furthermore, they have identified issues related to the three categories. Table IV outlines these issues.[3] They have found developmental stages for those seventeen issues. That gets very complicated. Table V summarizes all that work into a more useful form.[4]

Implications

What can be the meaning of Selman's theory to religious education? Or allow me to turn that question around

TABLE III.   SELMAN'S STAGES OF INTERPERSONAL
DEVELOPMENT

Codes:	Stages: Stage Titles:	Description of Stage: Interpersonal Relations and Kinds of Social Role-Taking	Age Range in C.A.:
0	Ego-Centric	Parallel play—difficulty in distinguishing between self and others.	03–06
1	Social-Infor-mational	Can see own perspective and one other person's, yet the main focus remains on self.	06–08
2	Self-Reflective	Sequential role-taking. Can understand self and other's perspective in concrete terms, but not simultaneously (e.g., "taking turns")	08–10
3	Mutual	Beginning of mutual role-taking, simultaneous process of self and others, but still largely concrete framework.	10–12
4	Social and Conventional Role-Taking	Awareness of subjective nature of interpersonal relations. Greater depth of feelings. Abstract and simultaneous perceptions. e.g., "The adolescent as a psychologist."	12–15

TABLE IV. ISSUES OF INTERPERSONAL AWARENESS RELATED
TO CONCEPTIONS OF THE INDIVIDUAL, CLOSE FRIENDSHIPS,
AND PEER-GROUP ORGANIZATION

Individual	Friendship	Peer Group
1. *Subjectivity:* covert properties of persons (thoughts, feelings, motives); conflicts between thoughts or feelings within the person	1. *Formation:* why (motives) and how (mechanisms) friendships are made; the idea of friend	1. *Formation:* why (motives) and how (mechanisms) groups are formed; the ideal member
2. *Self-Awareness:* awareness of the self's ability to observe its own thoughts and actions	2. *Closeness:* types of friendship, ideal friendship, intimacy	2. *Cohesion-Loyalty:* group unity
3. *Personality:* stable or predictive character traits	3. *Trust:* doing things for friends; reciprocity	3. *Conformity:* range and rationale
4. *Personality Change:* how and why people change (growing up)	4. *Jealousy:* feelings about intrusions into new or established relationships	4. *Rules and Norms:* types of rules and reasons for them
	5. *Conflicts:* how friends resolve problems	5. *Decision Making:* setting goals, resolving problems, working together
	6. *Termination:* how friendships break up	6. *Leadership:* its qualities and its function in the group
		7. *Termination:* why groups break up or members are excluded

TABLE V. GENERAL CHARACTERISTICS OF STAGES ACROSS CONCEPTIONS OF INDIVIDUALS, FRIENDSHIPS, AND PEER GROUPS

Stage	Individual	Friendship	Peer Group
0	Physical entity	Momentary physical playmate	Physical connections
1	Intentional subject	One-way assistance	Unilateral relations
2	Introspective self	Fair-weather cooperation	Bilateral partnerships
3	Stable personality	Intimate-mutual sharing	Homogeneous community
4	Complex self-systems	Autonomous interdependence	Pluralistic organization

slightly to ask, Is there a relationship between Selman's theory and values education?

In order to answer that question with a resounding "yes," I am going to discuss some lesson attitudes at several age levels for teaching the value of Christian love. Love is a many-splendored thing. I will only be addressing one component—sympathy, but the cummulative effect as we go from nursery to early adolescence will be evident.[5] I will discuss these lessons with respect to Selman's stages.

At the preschool level the lesson attitude is "learning to enjoy helping others have a good time." Preschool children have only momentary playmates and have difficulty distinguishing between self and others. The good time almost certainly means a self good time unrelated to others. But it is a step.

For grades 1 and 2 (6 and 7 years old) the lesson attitude is "learning to sympathize with those who are less fortunate." This may be possible with one person less fortunate, certainly not with less fortunate persons as a group.

For grades 3 and 4 (8 and 9 years old) the lesson attitude is "encouraging those who are experiencing failure." If experiencing failure is in very concrete terms 8 and 9 year olds can probably learn this attitude with one or two friends.

Moving to grades 7 and 8 (13 and 14 years old), the lesson attitude is "being friendly with children who are modestly endowed" (unattractive, clumsy, etc.). This would seem to be an excellent lesson for children moving from stage 3, mutual role taking in a homogenous community, to stage 4, social role taking in a pluralistic organization.

Moral Judgment

Moral judgment is closely related to interpersonal competencies. A moral judgment pertains to right and wrong. It is only right or wrong because moral judgments affect people and how people interrelate.

John Peatling

Lawrence Kohlberg is not the only researcher to study moral judgment. The "Kohlberg Bandwagon"[6] has overshadowed important work by Peatling. John Peatling[7] and Craig Dykstra[8] have both reviewed criticisms of Kohlberg's three level/six stage cognitive developmental theory. Criticizing Kohlberg is not my purpose. Rather I want to introduce Peatling's work for those of you who are unfamiliar with it.[9] His approach is quite different from

Kohlberg's. Whereas Kohlberg asserts that justice is unitary, Peatling went back to Piaget's *The Moral Judgment of the Child* in which Piaget described *five* aspects of the sense of justice.[10] So far Peatling has studied one aspect, equality and authority, although he has developed instruments for other aspects. Whereas Kohlberg confines himself to cognitive structure, Peatling measures the affective nature of moral judgment. Whereas Piaget confined his studies to school children, Peatling has studied children, adolescents, and adults.

Peatling's work began in the late 1960s when he first gathered data with *Thinking About the Bible*. You will recall that *Thinking About the Bible* is an instrument for measuring religious thinking. There are three stories for studying cognitive development. But there is also a fourth story for studying the development of relation to authority in a sense of justice.

The fourth is a story about a father and his two sons. The father goes away on a journey after telling his older son to watch his brother because his brother often does silly things. While the father is away the younger son does a silly thing. When the father comes home he asks the older son to report to him. The older son tells the father what his brother did.

The story is followed by questions with multiple choice responses which are criteria referenced to Piagetian responses of youngest, older, and oldest children. The questions are: What would you have done? Was the father fair? Would it be fair for the older son to lie? And what would be the nicest thing the older son could do?

Peatling's original data from around 2000 students nine years old to nineteen showed three stages which parallel Piaget's three stages in moral development. Nine, ten, and eleven year old children are in Stage 1. Twelve-, thirteen-, and fourteen-year-olds are in Stage 2. Stage 3 includes the older teenagers.

In terms of the aspect of justice about relation to authority, the stages can be described as follows:

Stage 1. (late childhood) A tendency toward submission to authority.

Stage 2. (early adolescents) A tendency toward keeping quiet in order to keep a friend out of trouble.

Stage 3. (late adolescents) A tendency to throw responsibility on to the accuser even though the accuser is an authority figure. Noncooperation in fault finding.

The three stages appear to be a progression from submission to authority through equity and equality to equalitarian solidarity.[11] However, a strange regression occurred with Peatling's adult sample which included seventy-nine persons involved in religious education who were fourteen to fifty-four years of age.[12] The school-age members were in Stage 3. The college-age members had dropped to Stage 2, while the post-college-age members had dropped to Stage 1. The climb back up to Stage II did not occur until the mid-forties. And a Stage III shift did not occur until the early fifties. This is a startling finding, particularly since this same sample, increasingly with age, progressed in abstract religious thinking.

Peatling speculates that his findings give us a clue to a macro-process of moral development. His life-span approach suggests that adults recycle through the same stages but at higher cognitive levels.[13]

Peatling has also done secondary analysis of his data looking for patterns of how people move from one stage to another. The work on the other four aspects of justice is incomplete. However, the work accomplished thus far is creative and fruitful. Peatling deserves a place in the annals of moral development.

Implications

Let us see what some lesson goals might be for that component of Christian love that can be called resolving conflicts. The value is channeling emotions for love rather than anger.[14]

The attitude for grades 5 and 6 reads, "Developing an understanding of why angry reactions to unfairness seldom solves the problem." Children in grades 5 and 6 still tend to submit to authority figures. When the authority figure is unfair this is probably a challenging lesson.

The attitude for grades 7 and 8 reads, "Faith that there are skills for turning the other cheek." This is an excellent lesson for young adolescents who want to keep quiet in order to protect a friend.

Finally, for grades 11 and 12 the attitude is, "A sense of personal responsibility for how people channel their emotions constructively." This appears to be highly idealistic for youth who tend toward noncooperation in fault finding. However, it would be a massive challenge. Christian values are, after all, a challenge to the best of us.

Let us take a look at the strategies we might use to teach such a lesson to students in grades 11 and 12. The class might begin with the teacher telling the story of the well-known singer, Marian Anderson, who was to give a concert in Washington, D.C. Because of her race, she was refused the only concert hall large enough for the audience she would draw. She reacted very graciously and sang before 75,000 people at the foot of the Lincoln Memorial. She said it was the most memorable occasion of her life. The following year she was awarded the Bok prize of $10,000 and used the entire sum to provide scholarships for struggling young musicians, regardless of class, creed, or color.[15]

The teacher might then discuss the meaning of magnanimity in conflict situations drawing on the experiences of class members. The class can list conflict situations and evaluate whether persons' contributions are creative, neutral, or negative. The class might role play some conflict situations. A home assignment could be diary records of conflict situations in the home, school, and neighborhood where the student's part is evaluated by her/him as creative, neutral, or negative.

The strategies are the presentation of a moral dilemma, discussion, real-life conflict situations, reflections on how emotions were channeled, role playing, and diary keeping all within the action-reflection model of learning. These abstract thinkers have been asked to use their reasoning powers, to take the perspective of others, to channel their emotions constructively for the good of all people concerned in conflict situations.

Moral judgment is involved in some decision making. However, not all decision making involves moral judgment. Thus, decision making can be treated separately. We move on to a decision-making theory.

Decision Making

Peatling has drawn our attention to the distinction between choice and decision. Choice "often is primarily impulsive, emotion-laden, essentially prerational or arational."[16] Deciding "is an act that often is primarily thoughtful, conscious, essentially rational."[17] He further posits that choosing is something that a young, maturing person does, whereas the mature individual engages more often in deciding. Here again is a developmental sequence. Even the most thoughtful, conscious, and rational decision-making systems still have at their heart the individual decision-maker's values.[18] Alternative actions, their predictability and probability, their consequences and risks involved are processed cognitively. However, all the information processing still has to coexist with the decider's values which are both cognitive and affective. Thus one's values system filters one's decisions. In understanding the whole learner, it would be helpful to discuss a decision-making theory. I present the theory of David Tiedeman.

David Tiedeman

David Tiedeman is well known in educational circles for his work in career education and decision making.[19] When educators today use the term career, they do not mean job training which is the province of vocational education. Career education is education for the beneficial use of one's whole life. This may be confusing to religious educators because we are apt to associate vocation (a calling) with the beneficial use of one's whole life. The religious meaning of vocation and educator's meaning of career have much in common.

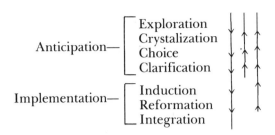

FIGURE 1.   THE TIEDEMAN-O'HARA PARADIGM OF CAREER
DECISION MAKING

I bring this similarity between vocation and career to
your attention because the Tiedeman-O'Hara paradigm is
a career decision-making paradigm.[20] The late Robert
O'Hara teamed with Tiedeman to produce the paradigm
in 1963. At that time, they were thinking in terms of job
decisions. However, Tiedeman continued to expound on
the paradigm and expand on the meaning of career. I am
going to suggest that the Tiedeman-O'Hara career decision-making paradigm has implications for *all* decision
making. I will be more specific by saying that the paradigm
is helpful for career decisions and religious conversion
decisions (if religious conversion can be called a decision
rather than a choice). Figure 1 gives the bare bones of the
Tiedeman-O'Hara paradigm.

The first thing to notice is the supracategories of Anticipation and Implementation. Any important decision
making has an in-the-head stage (anticipation) and then
the out-of-the-head stage (implementation). Consequences of one's decision involve people besides oneself.
Have you ever thought about decision making this way as a
religious person?

Exploration can be identified with the problem identification of the creative process.[21] It can also be identified with the career fantasies of preadolescents and early adolescents.

Crystalization is a kind of lining up of decision options leading to a choice of one option. Clarification is a kind of rationalizing that the choice was a good (right) choice.

All those stages prepare the individual to risk Implementation. An important decision, whether it is for a career or for a conversion, involves risk out there in the interpersonal world. You at first tentatively implement your choice. You have moved to *induction*. In career you have been accepted as a new employee. Now as you evaluate yourself in career you look around and see that some *reformation* is in order so that you can, in fact, be effective with your fellow employees and management. Finally you decide whether or not to *integrate* your career decision. You must make peace with your co-workers. You must decide whether the job position is best for you and others. It may not be. You must decide whether you will integrate or not.

The "or not" is the reason for all those directional arrows in Figure 1. You can start anywhere in the series of stages in Anticipation and go backward or forward. At any stage in Implementation before Integration you can go back to Anticipation. The implicit assumption is that the complete sequence will eventually be experienced.[22]

This is not a developmental theory in the sense that the other theories we have looked at are developmental. One stage does not build upon a prior stage in an invariant, irreversible sequence. The paradigm only applies to adolescents and adults. It applies to each decision. A person can be in Implementation stages with decision A but in Anticipation stages with decision B, or somewhat in between with decision C. However, the paradigm does help us understand how decisions are made and then implemented. It gives us another resource in understanding the whole learner.

Implications

When teachers understand the Tiedeman-O'Hara paradigm they will better be able to meet the needs of learners. Learners who are only at the exploration stage in any particular decision, need encouragement to seek information in the real world. Information is particularly important during the crystalization stage. After a choice has been made and learners are in a clarification stage, patience, understanding, and time are needed before induction can begin. Here learners need to understand the influence their decision has on other people. Responsibility for self and others is important and necessary for reformation and integration.

I recommend the use of the paradigm itself for a study group of adults. Let us say that the adults have determined to study that part of Christian hope that is career. The paradigm can help them determine where they are with any particular decision. Furthermore, it can help them see where they are going so that they can own their decisions and be responsible for them. The group could quickly become a self-help group, with members providing a listening ear for others or providing information for others as needed. Mid-life crises often become crises because stagnation occurs at some stage in the paradigm.[23] Group support and encouragement in a Christian community could help alleviate such crises. Members would be learning the value of hope together.

Two final developmental theories will be considered in the following chapter.

Chapter 8 Notes and References

1. Ellen Ward Cooney and Robert L. Selman, "Children's Use of Social Conceptions Towards a Dynamic Model of Social Cognition," in *New Directions for Child Development: Social Cognition* (San Francisco: Jossey-Bass, 1978).

2. Table 3 is taken from Norman A. Sprinthall's chapter, "A Primer on Development," in *Value Development . . . As the Aim of Education,* ed. Norman A. Sprinthall and Ralph L. Mosher (Schenectady, N.Y.: Character Research Press, 1978).

3. Cooney and Selman, p. 28.

4. Ibid., p. 29.

5. The attitudes are taken from the Social Potential Unit in the Character Research Project's *Research Curriculum,* Schenectady, N.Y.

6. Jack R. Frankel started the term "Kohlberg Bandwagon." His critique appears in *Readings in Moral Education,* ed. Peter Scharf (Minneapolis: Winston Press, Inc., 1978).

7. John H. Peatling, "A Sense of Justice: Moral Judgment in Children, Adolescents and Adults," *Character Potential: A Record of Research* 18(1) (November, 1976).

8. Craig Dykstra, *Vision and Character: A Christian Educator's Alternative to Kohlberg* (New York: Paulist Press, 1981).

9. Peatling's published research reports on moral development are the following:

"A Sense of Justice: Moral Judgment in Children, Adolescents and Adults," *Character Potential: A Record of Research* 18(1) (November, 1976). "Research on Adult Moral Development: Where Is It?" *Religious Education* LXXII (2) (March–April, 1977). "Five Cries From Mid-Life," *Character Potential* 8(3) (February, 1978). "A Sense of Justice: Responses of Finnish Students to a Piagetian Puzzle About Peer Protection and One's Relation to Authority," *Character Potential* 9(4) (1981).

10. Jean Piaget, *The Moral Judgment of the Child* (London: Kegan Paul, 1932). The other four aspects are: Punishment or retributive justice, collective/communicable responsibility, immanent justice, and distributive justice.

11. Peatling, "A Sense of Justice: Responses of Finnish Students. . . ," p. 234.

12. Peatling, "A Sense of Justice: Moral Judgment. . . ," pp. 25–34.

13. Ibid., p. 32.

14. The attitudes are taken from the Magnanimity Unit, of the Character Research Project's *Research Curriculum*. Schenectady, N.Y.

15. Ibid., Senior II, Lesson 4.

16. John H. Peatling, *Religious Education in a Psychological Key* (Birmingham, Ala.: Religious Education Press, 1981), p. 78.

17. Ibid., p. 79.

18. See Irwin D. J., Bross, *Design for Decision* (New York: Macmillan, 1953).

19. Tiedeman is president of the National Institute for the Advancement of Career Education at the University of Southern California.

20. David V. Tiedeman and Robert P. O'Hara, *Career Development: Choice and Adjustment* (New York: College Entrance Examination Board, 1963).

21. See Mary Henle's chapter, "The Birth and Death of Ideas," in *Contemporary Approaches to Creative Thinking* (New York: Atherton Press, 1962).

22. James E. Loder in describing the creative process allows that a person can enter his five point sequence at any point and go backwards and forwards. See "Transformation in Christian Education," *Religious Education* 76(2) (1981).

23. For reading about decisions in transition periods of life, I recommend *The Seasons of a Man's Life*, by Daniel J. Levinson et al. (New York: Ballantine Books, 1978).

CHAPTER 9

Self-Actualization and Ego-Development

There are two final strands that I will address in this chapter: the theories of Abraham Maslow and Jane Loevinger. Both theories are comprehensive and encompass the whole personality, not just cognitions, affectivity, interpersonal perspectives, moral judgment, or decision making.

Abraham Maslow

Abraham Maslow was a creative psychologist whose reputation peaked in 1962 when his classic book, *Toward a Psychology of Being*[1] was first published and when he was president of the American Psychological Association. He is rarely mentioned in the literature of religious education. I suspect that when religious educators began turning to psychology, Maslow was old hat. He was overlooked.

Thus, I want to go back to Maslow because he had important things to say to religious educators, as we shall see.

Until recently, psychologists for the most part followed the medical model. Diagnose the sickness and then cure. Maslow had quite a different approach. He believed that if you want to study healthy people you avoid pathologies and concentrate on the healthiest people. That makes good sense.

Maslow's most noteworthy contribution was his hierarchy of human needs. See Figure 2 below.

Psysiological needs such as for food, water, air, and sex are urgent basic needs. These needs must be met before safety needs can be attended to. The safety needs next to be met are freedom from illness, danger, and disruption of routines. If safety needs go unmet the child may become neurotic or psychotic. If safety needs are adequately met, the next level needs are for love, affection, and belonging. The child needs to give as well as receive love from individuals and from groups. If the love needs are thwarted, severe pathology may occur. If the love needs

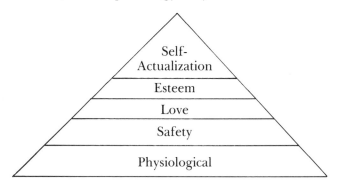

FIGURE 2.   MASLOW'S HIERARCHY OF NEEDS

are met, the way is open for the next level, the esteem needs. Individuals need competence, mastery, achievement, and recognition. Children or adults who have the physiological, the safety, and the love needs met but whose esteem needs go ignored become discouraged and depressed. The final growth motivation is to satisfy the needs for self-actualization.

Look at that triangle again. Try to see it as a dynamic process. Development is not a step by step climb up the ladder. There are slips and falls. Once the physiological and safety needs are met in infancy they continue to need meeting during the lifetime. If a nuclear bomb exploded and somehow you survived in devastated surroundings, you would be at the bottom of the ladder again. Your primary need would be for food and water, never mind safety, love, or esteem.

In our society most of us above the poverty level can climb the ladder to meet esteem needs or at least some esteem needs. Very few meet self-actualizing needs. Yet the potential is there. Of course self-actualizers do not spend all day, every day self-actualizing. They drop back to shore up love and esteem needs. Maslow's extreme interest was to learn all he could from persons who have had self-actualizing experiences.

Maslow believed that at the core of a person there is an inner need to self-actualize. Self-actualization is *being* the best that is humanly possible. Actually this is a religious idea and Maslow recognized this. Growth is *becoming*. Self-actualization is *being*. Maslow called it having B cognitions as opposed to D cognitions. D cognitions are organized around *deficiency* needs. People have D cognitions constantly in order to survive. B cognitions are different: they are good, right, uplifting, out of time and space, objective, and transcending.

B cognitions are related to B values of being. Self-actualizers in peak experiences adhere to these B values. The orientations to B values is being totally one's self but in a transformed way—more wholly self, beyond self. Jesus is an example of a self-actualized person. Here is Maslow's list of B values.[2] Have you known people who have lived within such a value system?

(1) wholeness
(2) perfection
(3) completion
(4) justice
(5) aliveness
(6) richness
(7) simplicity
(8) beauty
(9) goodness
(10) uniqueness
(11) effortlessness
(12) playfulness
(13) truth; honesty; reality
(14) self-sufficiency

Perhaps a discussion of B love and D love will clarify matters. B love is love for the being of another. It is unneeding love and unselfish love. D love on the other hand is deficiency love, needing love, and selfish love. D love is of the receiving kind while B love is of the giving kind. In B love the other is seen as a whole. Parts of that whole in and of themselves may be undesirable. Yet the whole is loved, the parts are transformed. B love is possible for only mature, self-actualizing people. A mother's love for her baby is a common example. She may and often does demonstrate B love. The baby's health and welfare come before the mother's self. She would give up her life for her child if need be. Her baby may be ugly—that hardly matters. As baby and mother stare deeply into each other's eyes time and place stand still. This is a peak experience. It is good and right, joyful and self-actualizing. B love is a potential for all. With B love in mind look at Maslow's values again. Do not those values describe the peak experience between mother and baby? Do not they also describe Jesus' life?

Maslow believed that the potential for self-actualization lies within each one of us. We need to self-actualize. Religion should help people fill that need and be their best selves. Religious education should have as one of its goals self-actualized persons.

"I think it fair to say that no theory of psychology will ever be complete which does not centrally incorporate the concept that man has his future within him, dynamically active at this present moment."[3] To get a further flavor of Maslow try this idea. "At the level of self-actualizing many dichotomies become resolved, opposites are seen to be unities and the whole dichotomous way of thinking is recognized to be immature."[4] No wonder I include Maslow. He believed that apparent opposites can be transcended. He believed in potential.

Implications from Maslow

Next we will look at a Values Education program,[5] while at the same time testing that program against Maslow's pyramid of needs. Remember that the developmental levels are not found in Maslow's theory in the same way as they are found in invariant stage theories. Depending on the environment and what is provided for physiological needs and safety needs, teachers can attend to love and esteem needs and finally self-actualizing needs. Learners can be climbing steadily or may temporarily slip back.

Teachers must understand the whole learner and assess where learners are in their development toward self-actualization. Teachers must teach to developmental level.

The ultimate value is faith in God. We can teach children attitudes which will contribute to faith in God. Yet we must understand that we are engaged in a long-term process.

Ages 2–3. "A growing confidence in parents because of the many ways they help the child" is the attitude. This lesson is a first step and meets a love need. It also demonstrates the importance of family and the importance of training parents so that they can teach their children.

Ages 4–5. "Developing a desire to learn the way a Father God cares for us" is the attitude. We have moved up from parents to God. These children can only intuitively recognize God. The lesson(s) would fulfill the love needs of these preoperational children.

Grades 1 and 2. "Recognizing that we can learn God's laws" is the attitude. Children seem to need an authority figure, and this God can be to them. However, their conceptions of God are apt to be quite anthropomorphic.[6] Love needs are met and esteem needs are somewhat met. Learning God's laws require some competencies which are relatively new to the child.

Grades 3 and 4. "A growing understanding of how to work with God." This lesson is one more step along a long path. It fulfills love and esteem needs.

Grades 5 and 6. "Faith in a Father God whose will is a source of great power" is the attitude. At 4 and 5 years of age the lesson is a *desire* lesson. At grades 1 and 2 the lesson is a *recognition* lesson. Grades 3 and 4 receive an *understanding* lesson. Now, at grades 5 and 6, the children get their first *faith* lesson.

Grades 7 and 8. "Faith in a Father God whose will consists of social-spiritual laws" is the attitude. Love and esteem needs are still met. However, this is a basic, foundational lesson in self-actualizing. Mastering the social-spiritual laws must relate to the potential in humans.

Senior High School. "Developing a mature concept of being a son of God, implying that choice of vocation, acceptance of social responsibilities, and the extent and nature of educational preparation must be based on learning and doing God's will." Learning and doing God's will and developing a mature concept of being a child of God is a religious way of expressing B love and facilitating self-actualizing experiences.

The attitudes mentioned above appear to dovetail nicely with Maslow's needs hierarchy. They represent a developmental progression from preschool through high school which should contribute to the learning of the value, faith.

Loevinger[7]

The final strand in our Golden Braid is the theory of Jane Loevinger on ego-development. Loevinger is not talking about Freudian development of the id, the ego, and the super-ego. Her theory transcends psychoanalysis and reinterprets. Her theory is encompassing in that it includes

TABLE VI. LOEVINGER'S "MILESTONES" OF EGO
DEVELOPMENT

Stage:	Code:	Impulse Control, and/or Character Development:
Presocial	I–1	
Symbiotic		
Impulsive	I–2	Impulsive, fear of retaliation.
Self-Protective	Δ	Fear of being caught, externalizing blame, opportunistic.
Conformist	I–3	Conformity to external rules, shame, guilt for breaking rules.
Conscientious	I–4	Self-evaluated standards, self-criticism, guilt for consequences, long-term goals and ideals.
Autonomous	I–5	(In addition to Level I–4, *add*) Coping with conflicting inner needs, toleration.
Integrated	I–6	(In addition to Level I–5, *add*) Reconciling inner conflicts, renunciation of unattainable.

character development, moral development, socialization, and cognitive development. Her purpose is structuring.

First I would like to give you a simple outline of Loevinger's stages.

Later she expanded this table by additional columns. The right hand column in Table VI above she named, Impulsive Control and/or Character Development. Then she added three more columns, namely Interpersonal Style, Conscious Preoccupations, and Cognitive Style. I am going to describe each stage so that the remaining three columns are included.

Presocial Stage (I-1) and Symbiotic Stage (I-1)

A baby at birth has no sense of self. The baby must differentiate self from the environment. She/he does this by learning object constancy, meaning that objects remain constant even though they are removed from sight. A nine-month-old baby begins to learn that mother and toys although unseen are constant. The interpersonal style of the child who does not attain this presocial stage is autistic.

The baby who has learned object constancy is still in a symbiotic relation with the mother or whoever is the primary caretaker. The development of language helps the child to further recognize self as separate from others. The conscious preoccupation of the symbiotic stage is self vs. nonself.

Impulsive State (I-2)

The impulsive stage is evidenced by "No," "Me Mean It," and "Do it Byself." Some have named this stage the "terrible twos." The child has recognized self as separate from others but does not yet know what the self is. The dependence-independence struggle is apparent. There is fear of retaliation from adults. The child is dependent and exploitive. The child is fighting for independence at a time when bodily feelings are excessive. This leads to conceptual confusion about self.

Self-Protective Stage (Delta A)

This is a first step in controlling impulses. Rules begin to be acknowledged. The basic rule is "Don't get caught." Blame is not put on self (in self-protection), it is placed outside self or on an imaginary friend. Conscious preoccupations center on trouble, wishes, advantage, and control. Exploitive describes the interpersonal style. Some older children remain at this stage. Opportunist hedonism describes them.

Conformist Stage (I-3)

The child begins to identify her/his own interests with that of the group. This is a step forward in ego development. At the previous stage competition was present for control. Now the behavior of cooperation is apparent. Individuals at this stage obey rules because they are group norms. The concept of consequences of behavior is ignored. The desirability of being socially acceptable by the group is all-important. Since belonging is a goal, stereotyping and cliches are common.

Self-Aware Level: Transition from Conformist to Conscientious Stage (I3/4)

This stage does not show up on Table VI. It is a transition level. However since it is the modal level for adults, it begs description. The two ways in which this level differs from the Conformist Stage are (1) an increase in self-awareness and (2) an appreciation of the multiple possibilities in situations. The cognitive style now becomes "multiplicity." Loevinger does not name this a stage, only a transition between stages. It is a breaking away from Conformitivity but not yet truly Conscientious.

Conscientious Stage (I-4)

A person at this stage has a conscience. Whereas a Conformist would not blame self, a Conscientious person would. Whereas a Conformist would not take responsibility for consequences, a Conscientious person would. Moreover, a Conscientious person will break rules depending on how she/he judges a situation. Conceptual complexity is possible at this stage. Mutuality in interpersonal relations is also possible now.

Individualistic Level: Transition from Conscientious to Autonomous Stages (I-4/5)

Persons at this level have a heightened sense of individuality and a concern for emotional dependence. Individuality of self and others is respected. Distinctions are made between process and outcome. There is a differentiation of inner life from outer life.

Autonomous Stage (I-5)

Persons at this stage can acknowledge and cope with inner conflict. They transcend polar opposites and see reality as complex and multifaceted. There is high toleration for ambiguity. The need by others for autonomy is recognized and accepted. There is greater objectivity.

Integrated State (I-6)

So few adults reach this stage that it is difficult to define it. The interpersonal style is cherishing of individuality. "Probably the best description of this stage is that of Maslow's Self-Actualizing person."[10]

Sprinthall has gathered data on the Loevinger scale and gives us age ranges.[11] Table VII gives his very rough estimates.

What this surely should tell us is that adults have not completed their maturity. They continue to develop in at least cognitions (Peatling), their moral judgments (Peatling), decision making (Tiedeman), needs (Maslow), and their ego development (Loevinger). Development continues until death. Religious education with adults still involves learners who can attain greater and greater amounts of potential.

Implications from Loevinger

The point I made about teaching to developmental level becomes crucial. Let us suppose that we are to be facilita-

TABLE VII. MY EXTRAPOLATIONS FOR LOEVINGER'S EGO
DEVELOPMENT STAGES FROM SPRINTHALL

Loevinger Stages	Code	Sprinthall's Extrapolations
Presocial	I–1	
Impulsive	I–2	Elementary School
Self Protective	△	
Conformist	I–3	Teenagers and young
Conscientious	I–4	adults
Autonomous	I–5	A very few mature
Integrated	I–6	adults

tors of a young adult group who are about to study the value of Christian love. Part of Loevinger's theory has to do with cognitive style. Her stages go from conceptual confusion to increased conceptual complexity. Table VIII simplifies the stages from the point of view of cognitive style.

Sprinthall's data led him to believe that the modal point for adults lies in the transition between conformist and conscientious (Stage 1-3/4). Thus in our group of young (18-24 years) adults,[13] it would be well to know at what stage each learner is in ego development. Suppose a learner is at the conformist stage. It would be unwise to expect movement from conformity to autonomy. No, we must go a step at a time in a long-term process. We must so arrange the environment so that we can facilitate growth toward conscientious-conformity. Loevinger does have a test which provides sentence stems and a manual for coding. It would be well to measure the stage of ego development before any teacher-learner interaction begins.

Very likely any group of young adults will contain people at various stages. The teacher as facilitator in an open-

TABLE VIII. LOEVINGER'S STAGES AND LEVELS WITH
ACCOMPANYING COMPLEXITY DESCRIPTION[12]

Stage	Cognitive Style
Impulsive	Stereotyping, conceptual confusion
Self-Protective	
Conformist	Conceptual simplicity, stereotypes, cliches
Conscientious-Conformist	Multiplicity
Conscientious	Conceptual complexity, idea of patterning
Individualistic	Add: Distinction of process and outcome
Autonomous	Increased conceptual complexity, complex patterns, toleration for ambiguity, broad scope, objectivity

ended system provides a moral dilemma problem (in this case, concerning Christian love) and asks the group to discuss resolutions. The mixture of different stages among the learners works to advantage; higher-level thinkers stimulate lower-level thinkers to move up a stage. For the conformist learner there is a long way to go. Thus, a long-term process is involved.

We have spoken about the importance of family and community. For the preschool child, the family is the community. The parents are the teachers. Then, as children grow up, the church parish becomes a community as does the school community. Young adults are attempting to break free of their family and become independent. The break is seldom complete. However, other communities become dominant. The study group becomes a community, particularly in the study of Christian love.

The importance of teacher training is crucial. As a facilitator, the teacher must know each learner as a whole person so that she/he can be sensitive to each learner's development. The teacher must assist learners to use an action-reflection model of learning. Ideally, the teacher can also become a learner with the group.[14]

Summary

We have looked at the theories of Maslow on self-actualization and Loevinger on ego development. We have considered implications of these theories for religious education. Along the way, the fourteen points for successful values education have been considered. These accomplishments have been relatively easy when dealing with only one or two theories at a time. However, we have been building toward a Golden Braid. What happens when we put all nine strands together? The development of the whole learner and the implications for values education follow in chapter 10.

Chapter 9 References and Footnotes

1. Abraham M. Maslow, *Toward a Psychology of Being* (Princeton: P. Van Nostrand, 1962).

2. Abraham M. Maslow, *The Farther Reaches of Human Nature* (New York: Viking Press, 1971), pp. 133–135.

3. Maslow, *Toward a Psychology of Being*, p. 14.

4. Ibid., p. 192.

5. The attitudes are my revisions of the Character Research Project's Universe Unit.

6. See David Elkind, *The Child's Reality: Three Developmental Themes* (Hillsdale, N.J.: Lawrence Erlbaum Associates, 1978), and two monographs by V. Peter Pitts, *The God Concept in the Child* and *Children's Pictures of God* (Schenectady, N.Y.: Character Research Press, 1977 and 1979, respectively).

7. Jane Loevinger, *Ego Development* (San Francisco: Jossey-Bass Publishers, 1980).

8. Taken from *Value Development . . . As the Aim of Education,* ed. Norman A. Sprinthall and Ralph L. Mosher (Schenectady, N.Y.: Character Research Press, 1978), p. 10.

9. Loevinger, *Ego Development,* p. 24, 25.

10. Ibid., p. 26, and also see Ibid., p. 140.
   "The physiological needs correspond to the Presocial and Impulsive Stages; the need for safety corresponds to the Self-Protective Stage; needs for love and belonging corresponds to the Conformist Stage; needs for respect and self-esteem correspond to the Conscientious Stage; self-actualization corresponds to the Autonomous and Integrated Stages."

11. Sprinthall, "A Primer on Development" in *Value Development . . . As the Aim of Education,* p. 11.

12. This table is adapted for our purposes from a large chart, p. 24 and 25, in Loevinger's *Ego Development.*

13. I am assigning ages 18 through 24 as "young adults." I do this based on empirical evidence in Merton Strommen et al., *A Study of Generations* (Minneapolis, Augsburg Publishing House, 1972).

14. Leon McKenzie, *The Religious Education of Adults* (Birmingham, Ala., Religious Education Press, 1982).

CHAPTER 10

The Golden Braid and a Maypole Dance

My purpose in introducing the nine theories in the past three chapters was, of course, to keep the focus on: 1) development, 2) understanding the whole learner, and 3) on teaching to developmental level. As we have seen, these are very important aspects in teaching values. The developmental aspects are not the only important ones in teaching values. However, I wish to continue with development, because the more we know about development, the better religious educators we will be. God has given us a tremendous clue to patterns in creation which, if we use rather than ignore, can help us to be better teachers.[1]

My task in this chapter is to take the nine strands and braid them into a Golden Braid. We will accomplish the Golden Braid with a Maypole dance. Then we will look at cross sections of the Braid at different developmental levels in order to better understand the levels and, finally, to understand implications for values education. Your task will not be easy. Integration of titles of stages at any developmental level probably will require your review of chapters 7, 8 and 9. Furthermore, my Golden Braid contains only nine strands. I have not included Erikson, Fowler, Havighurst, Kohlberg, and others whom you may want to include on your own.

At any cross section of our Golden Braid, you will not necessarily see all nine strands. The reason is simple. The Tiedeman-O'Hara paradigm does not apply to preschoolers or elementary school pupils. Peatling's data was not collected from any pupils below fourth grade. Perry's theory does not apply to any below adolescence. Dupont's and Piaget's affectivity theories do not appear to differentiate adult stages. Be that as it may, any decisions on designating developmental levels by chronological age need explanation. For the rest of this book, these are the developmental levels I will address:

2-5 years	Preschool
6-11 years	Elementary School
12-15 years	Early Adolescence
16-28 years	Youth & Early Adult
50 years	Adulthood

There is nothing exceptional about the Preschool Level or the Elementary School Level. These approximate Piaget's preoperational and concrete operational thinking stages. Focusing on four years as Early Adolescence may seem exceptional. However, I name Selman, Peatling, and Sprinthall's work with ego development data as my rationale. Moreover, as we go along I believe you will see enough differences between the 12-15 years level and the

16-28 years level to warrant assigning Early Adolescence as a separate developmental level.

My 16-28 years developmental level may come as a surprise. It is a compromise. I started with Merton Strommen's *Study of Generations*.[2] He found that his first generation was 15-29. He further was able to designate three subgenerations: 15-18, 19-23, and 24-29.[3] Daniel Levinson took a different view in *The Seasons of a Man's Life*.[4] However, there appears a similarity. Up until 17 he designates as Childhood and Adolescence, 17-22 as Early Adult Transition, and 22-28 as Entering the Adult World.[5]

Next I thought about Gilligan's work with 19-27-year-olds on Perry's scale and Peatling's work with an adult sample on cognitive and moral judgment development. Certainly development does not cease with graduation from high school. Something interesting is happening as youth adjust to the adult world. The difficulty is that not a great deal is definitively known yet about adult development.

Naomi Golan has done us a service in her book, *Passing Through Transitions*.[6] She spends an entire chapter reviewing many authors' thoughts about adult development including Jung, Buhler, Erikson, Havinghurst, Neugarten, Duvell, Levinson, Gould, Lowenthall, and Sheehy.[7] My conclusion after reading her review is that an arbitrary decision must be made among numerous choices if we are to proceed in any practical sense. I have made mine: 16-28 years is a developmental level. This is not to say that I am correct. And it certainly is no recommendation that further research is unnecessary. Further research is necessary. I predict that a decade from now we will have broken down the 16-28 level into definitive levels within that range, perhaps as Strommen has suggested.

My last, most mature, level is 30-59 years. Adulthood, is another compromise. Very little is known about adults over 60. Who knows when maturity is achieved, or, for that matter what maturity is! Thus, I will be talking about the 50s as my most mature level. This is an arbitrary decision. On the one hand, I have no evidence that 50 year olds are mature. On the other hand, I do not wish to get into the declining years of Havighurst's 60s.[8]

A Maypole Dance

Imagine if you will a maypole with nine ribbons streaming down from the top. Nine maypole dancers are beginning their dance. Some dance in one direction, some in the other direction. The dance weaves the strands from top to bottom until at the completion of the dance we have the Golden Braid woven around the maypole. The braid woven around the maypole represents the whole learner. The pole itself represents the Self, the core of Rokeach's system of beliefs. We can look at cross sections of our braid at particular developmental levels. Our first level is Preschool. Here is a listing of titles of developmental stages for the Preschool level.

Preschool

Title	Theorist	Type of Development
Heteronomous	Dupont	Affective
Intuitive Affects	Piaget	Affective
Preoperational	Piaget	Cognitive
Egocentric	Selman	Interpersonal
Physiological, Safety, Love Needs	Maslow	Needs
Impulsive, Self-Protection	Loevinger	Ego Development

This set of stage titles suggests a vulnerability in Pre-school children. They are dependent on parents for fulfilling their physiological and safety needs. They are so wrapped up in themselves that they have little idea about the perspectives of others. They neither think nor feel like adults. They lack experiences. They stumble along on intuition.

6-11 Years

In this list of stage titles, you will see 1, 2, 3, and 4 stages depending on the author concerned and her/his theory. This suggests a great deal of movement during these important years.

Title	Theorist	Type of Development
Heteronomous and Inter-personal	Dupont	Affective
Intuitive and Normative Affects	Piaget	Affective
Intuitive and Firmly Concrete	Peatling	Cognitive
Social-Information, Self-Reflective and Mutual	Selman	Interpersonal
Submission to Authority	Peatling	Moral
Physiological, Safety, Love, and Esteem	Maslow	Needs
Impulsive, Self-Protective, and Conformist	Loevinger	Ego Development

The movement appears to involve a shift from intuitive, impulsive, and submission toward recognition of the peer group and one's concrete relation to norms.

12-15 Years

Here are the stage titles of Early Adolescence.

Title	Theorist	Type of Development
Interpersonal	Dupont	Affective
Idealistic Feelings	Piaget	Affective
Early Abstract	Peatling	Cognitive
Social and Conventional Role Taking	Selman	Interpersonal
Keep Quiet to Protect a Friend	Peatling	Moral
Exploration	Tiedeman	Decision Making
Esteem and Self-Actualizing	Maslow	Needs
Self-Protective and Conformist	Loevinger	Ego Development

My description of the weave at this level would suggest a holding position of safety in the peer group while abstract thinking is in its early stages, while explorations in career and while self-actualizing experiences are potentials. This is a tentative period compared to the explosion of the 16-28 year level. The following are the stage titles for the next level.

16-28 Years

Title	Theorist	Type of Development
Personal-autonomous	Dupont	Affective
Idealistic Feelings	Piaget	Affective
Abstract	Peatling	Cognitive

Title	Theorist	Type of Development
Multiplicity, Relativism, and Commitment	Perry	Cognitive
Autonomous Interdependence	Selman	Interpersonal
Assigning Responsibility	Peatling	Moral
Choice, Clarification, Induction, and Reformation	Tiedeman	Decision Making
Esteem and Self-Actualizing	Maslow	Needs
Autonomous and Integrated	Loevinger	Ego Development

Those titles suggest an independent and interdependent person, one who begins to self-actualize and begins integration. The titles also suggest an objectivity about reality and the ability to handle complexities. Finally these titles describe a maturity religious educators might wish for all learners in religious education.

The sad fact is, of course, that only a few adults reach the heights that are potentially theirs. Most adults are at Loevinger's Self-Awareness level between the Conformist and the Conscientious Stages. Few adults are experienced in self-actualizing, and few reach Loevinger's Autonomous or Integrated Stages. Peatling found regression to an elementary school level in moral judgment for students in their twenties. Many adults never progress beyond Piaget's Normative Feelings. Perry found few college seniors who were firmly at the Commitment position.

I can think of three reasons for this sad state of affairs. First, there is the possibility that development has been repressed during earlier stages, that is to say that the environment discouraged development in childhood. Second, the environment the adolescent enters in her or his twenties rewards conformity and does not reward autonomy. Finally, a combination of past experience and young adult experience stands in the way of development.

It is beyond the scope of this book to get into the matter of genetic impairment as a reason for adults being locked into immature stages of development. Yet that is a possibility. However, the generalization can be made that all children of God have unrealized potential. Everyone, even the impaired, can progress in religious development. The religious educator must determine where each learner, child, adolescent, or adult, is developmentally and then proceed a step at a time toward a higher stage or level.

50-Year-Olds

The Maypole Dance is not yet complete. Development does not end at 28 years of age. The bottom half of the pole has not been braided yet. Let us continue the weaving dance. Now we are clearly into adult education. I am going to interrupt in the decade of the fifties, not because the dance is completed, but because we know so little about our older people.

Title	Theorist	Type of Development
Commitment in Relativism	Perry	Cognitive
Very Abstract	Peatling	Cognitive
Equalitarian	Peatling	Moral

Title	Theorist	Type of Development
Integration	Tiedeman	Decision Making
Self-Actualizing	Maslow	Needs
Integrated	Loevinger	Ego Development

With such stage titles, we seem to have gone beyond the 16-28-year-old's battle for autonomy. We seem to have progressed to integration of all development heretofore which would include respect for others, an objectivity toward oneself and others, plus a commitment in relativism.

It is difficult to write about stage 6 because there are so few examples. The great majority of us are just not there yet. At the very best, stage 6 is an ultimate goal. At the very least, parts of stage 6 can be ultimate goals. We can help older people to use their cognitive powers in more and more abstract ways by continual cognitive challenges. We can help adults in their moral judgments by exposure to scriptural passages which emphasize the equality of all human beings. We can help adults with decision making which emphasizes the responsibility of each individual to her/himself and others in the implementation of decisions. So far, I have addressed myself to cognition (Peatling-Very Abstract), moral judgment (Peatling-Equalitarian), and decision making (Tiedeman-Integration). What about commitment to Relativism (Perry), a Self-Actualization (Maslow), and Integrated (Loevinger)?

Commitment in Relativism

Perry's progress from Multiplicity, through Relativism, and on to Commitment in Relativism appears to me to have some relation to an adult who realizes the multiplicity and stops there, totally confused. Or, the adult can solve Multiplicity by espousing Relativism and leaves it there. "Everything is relative to everything else. So I accept that and try to live with it." What a challenge to a religious educator! Can that relativistic learner be moved on to Commitment in Relativisim? I believe that the answer is yes. If the teacher espouses values education Commitment in Relativism is a values education goal. It has to do with the value of hope. It has to do with education within a community of hopeful Christians.

Self-Actualization and Integration

I put these two terms together not because they must be together. Children can have self-actualizing experiences although they are hardly integrated in the Loevinger sense. An older integrated adult may never have experienced self-actualization. However, a mature adult who is well integrated, who can reconcile inner conflicts, and who is committed in relativism, it seems to me, can be more freely open to peak experiences than a less mature adult who is fighting for autonomy.

Implications of the Golden Braid for Religious Education

Now that we know more about learners at five developmental levels, let us look again at the cross sections of the Golden Braid and see what they can tell us about values education within religious education.

Preschool

Ronald Goldman calls preschool children "prereligious" in *Readiness for Religion*.[9] This does not mean that their religious education should not begin. Their religious education from their parents most certainly should begin as early as possible. Taking our orientation from values education helps clarify the importance of an early beginning. By the time children are five, they have already learned hundreds of attitudes. These attitudes will structure their values in ensuing years.

In *The Religious Education of Preschool Children* I have demonstrated seven instructional objectives for teaching the values of faith, hope, and love.[10] The objectives are appropriate to the developmental level. The child can learn to:

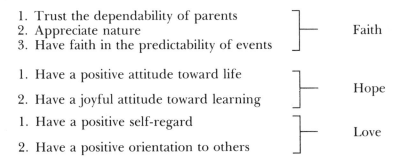

1. Trust the dependability of parents
2. Appreciate nature   Faith
3. Have faith in the predictability of events

1. Have a positive attitude toward life
                                                  Hope
2. Have a joyful attitude toward learning

1. Have a positive self-regard
                                                  Love
2. Have a positive orientation to others

Since preschoolers depend so heavily on their parents, it is the parents' responsibility to teach Christian values. They can teach values by using the principles of operant conditioning to reinforce desired behavior. Negative behavior is ignored. A loving community within the family is achieved. A long-term process is begun.

Parishes should provide training for their parents so that parents acquire greater understanding of their learners. Another aspect for which parents need training has to do with the gradual shift from operant conditioning to "intrinsic conditioning."

Children as young as three take pride in their achievements. Pride in this sense is not the kind that goes before a fall. It is more like joy in being able to achieve something (e.g., making a grand tower or learning to pump themselves on a swing). Such pride is a potential "intrinsic reinforcer." Success is a potential "intrinsic stimulus" challenging the child to build another tower or swing again on the swings.

"Intrinsic conditioning" motivates the self-directed learner. The basics for "intrinsic conditioning" can be formed during the preschool years. Further progress can be made during the elementary years.

6-11 Years

As we have seen, this developmental level includes several stages of development. Goldman talks about these children as "subreligious."[12] Be that as it may, developmentally they are in a latency period. They are building strength, as it were, for a burst of development in the teenage years in religion. They must move from dependence on family to security within their peer group. They must include among authority figures, not only parents, but also teachers, the clergy, policemen, Scout leaders, librarians, and others. They must learn social skills appropriate to their developmental stage in social perspective taking. As teachers rearrange the environment in order to provide maximum learning opportunities, teachers must make every effort to present materials so that lessons are geared to concrete thinking. Materials must relate to the everyday reality which is the child's world. Goldman has suggested themes (such as home, family, bread) for elementary school children.[13] Take the theme, bread, as an example. Elementary school children cannot understand, "this bread is my body which is broken for you." But they can understand a loaf of bread from the supermarket. They can understand what it means to have their class bake bread and eat it. The bread made in Sunday School sustains and nourishes them. This is a solid step and an honest one. The strategy is an illustration of the action-reflection model of learning within a loving community.

12-15 Years

This developmental level is crucial for religious education. I have called this a tentative period of security within the peer group, while physical changes of puberty take place and concrete thinking gives way to abstract thinking. This is a kind of buffer zone between childhood and pre-adulthood. On the one hand, allow these youngsters time—do not push them. But on the other hand, provide stimulating opportunities for learning about things religious that they want to discuss and analyze. Probably the worst mistake to make with early teenagers is to treat them like children. It is important to treat them like the self-motivated learners they can be. Help them recognize their own intrinsic motivation. If your learners at this developmental level can achieve self-motivation, their esteem needs will be filled, and they may even be on their way to self-actualization. Religious experiences at this level are not uncommon.[14]

The warnings are to go slowly, and do not try to break up a peer group. Peer group values are being tested, as they should be. All things being favorable, these early teenagers will return to family values or their own renditions of family values in late teenage years or in early adulthood.[15]

Will our early teenagers be turned on or turned off? This is a question which religious educators must address particularly at the parish level. An understanding of developmental levels will help make our approach more realistic and loving.

16-28 Years

The importance of peer group gradually diminishes. Family is again important but so are other people in college and the workplace as these youth engage in the battle for their own autonomy. The late teenage years are the years when Erikson says young people struggle with identity vs. role diffusion.[16] Since religion is strongly associated with identity for many, religious education must provide strong cognitive challenges for these abstract thinkers. We must help these young people gain self-confidence as they deal with multiplicities in our society.

Young people, in these dozen or more years, must not only deal with identity, they must also deal with career and, perhaps, marriage. Religious educators as facilitators and counselors can help young people with the concept of career as "calling." It is also our responsibility to offer "preparation for marriage" to these young people. These developmental aspects put religious educators in touch

with the needs of this developmental level. The 16-28 period is a crucial time for religious education.

Unfortunately, in most parishes, the 16-28-year-olds are
few and far between. We lose potential Christians when
they are either early or late teenagers. I submit that we lose
them because of our insufficient understanding of development and of teaching to developmental stage. Perhaps
we also lose teenagers because we allow well-meaning volunteer teachers to lead them when many of these volun-
teers are at immature levels of development.[17] We must
pay attention to the developmental stages of teachers as
well as students.

Many of us believe that drop-outs return in their 30s. A
recent study indicates that the returning age is earlier,
around 26 years of age.[18] Today we are dealing with
young people from the baby boom following World War
II. We could be talking about significant numbers. No
matter if the number is 1, 25, or 150, we must be ready.
These are the parents of the next generation of Christians.
What values will they transmit to their children? What
parenting education can we make available to our young
parents?

50-Year-Olds

I am not using 50 years old as a developmental level,
because as I have pointed out we know little about adult
development. Rather I am using it as a representative age
when maturity in our nine strands *may* be achieved. As
soon as I artificially erect an age (50) as an age when maturity in the nine strands may be achieved, I want to counter
by exposing the fallacy of the Stage 6s. Not an easy task.
But it is one well worth the effort for religious educators to

understand. Moreover, I can start with one of our own, James Loder. For the time being, let us leave Stage 6s in developmental theories (Piaget, Kohlberg, Loevinger, and Fowler) and attend to Loder's meaning of "transformation." In Loder's words, "transformation is the major term, designating a change in form from lower to higher orders of life along a continuous line of intention or development."[19] The clue for us here is "a change in form from lower to higher orders of life."

What might this change in form mean? As an introduction, Loder speaks of five steps in "transformational logic" or "knowing as a transformational event."[20] The first step is conflict as "an apparent rupture in the knowing context."[21] The second step is "an interlude of scanning" or "searching out of possible solutions."[22] The third step is "the constructive act of the imagination: an insight, intuition, or vision appears on the border between the conscious and unconscious."[23] This is like the "aha" solution. "It is by this central act that the elements of the ruptured situation are transformed, and a new perception, perspective, or world view is bestowed on the knower."[24]

The fourth step in transformational logic is "a release of energy" and an "opening up of the knower."[25] The final step is "interpretation of the imaginative solution into the behavioral and/or symbolically constructed world of the original context."[26] A transformation from a lower order to a higher level has occurred.

Loder goes on to describe what may be for him a Stage 6, although he does not allow himself to be limited to stage language. Loder points out a four-dimensional "knowing event" which includes knowledge of: 1) the lived world, 2) the self, 3) the void, and 4) the holy.[27] Within such multiple knowing, he introduces "convictional knowledge."

"Convictional knowing is the patterned process by which the Holy Spirit transforms all transformations of the human spirit. This is a four-dimensional, knowing event initiated, mediated, and concluded by Christ."[28]

Loder does not deny that human development proceeds in stages. His purpose is to insist that human transformations go only so far and that ultimately, for religious people, the Holy Spirit transforms. One clue to the divine, analogically, are transformations and our openness to them. The final stage is God's.

This may well be the way to go. It avoids the "fallacy of the Stage 6s." Loder's thoughts are difficult to comprehend. Developmentalists still tend to describe a most mature or Stage 6 level. Loevinger admits to difficulties in describing her Stage 6.[29] Kohlberg has recently retreated from his Stage 6.[30] In his recent book, *Stages of Faith*, Fowler demonstrates his awareness of criticisms that can be leveled against his Stage 6, "Universalizing Faith."[31] Piaget who knew about Gödel's theorem believed that his Stage 6, Formal Operations, was not the end-all in adult cognition.[32]

Gödel's theorem and James Loder's transformations, then, are the entrees to the "fallacy of the Stage 6s." Loder defines transformations as "changes in form from lower to higher orders of life." Stage 1 is transformed into Stage 2. Stage 2 is transformed into Stage 3, and so forth, in developmental theories. Gilligan and Murphy help us see the "fallacy of the Stage 6s" (a *highest* stage) by reviewing researchers' and theorists' reaction to Gödel's theorem.[33] I will try to simplify. Gödel was a mathematician who proved that in any system (say a developmental stage) the proof of that system does not exist. What we do is go to a higher system (transform to a next high stage or higher order). This works well enough until we come up against a Stage 6 (a highest stage or order). According to Gödell, the contradictions within a Stage 6 require an even higher system for explanation of truth.

The practical consequences which Gilligan and Murphy draw to our attention are the incompleteness of formal reasoning as the ultimate stage in cognitive development and the incompleteness of justice as the ultimate stage in moral development.[33] Perhaps the most we can do in transformations beyond Stage 5 is to recognize our incomplete understandings and at least leave formal reasoning and replace it or extend it to learning how adults behave in *real life* situations. Thus thinking incorporates affections and morality incorporates responsibility to others as well as self. Reasoning and justice are transformed in adult experience.

Let us then beware of the "fallacy of the Stage 6s" and look at implications for adult religious education. We do not know what maturity means. We have clues from the developmentalists and the goal of convictional knowing from Loder. Also, we have "conversion" from Gillespie and the disciplines of repentance, prayer, and service from Dykstra.[34] We have process theology from Miller and developmentalism from Wilcox.[35] Also, we have religious instruction from Lee and socialization from Westerhoff.[36] What do the Golden Braid and our other sources tell us about teaching values to adults?

Since I do not claim to be an expert in adult religious education, I am not going to pretend to be one. What I can do is to refer to the points I made in chapter 6 on what seemed to be successful facets of values education and then apply these to adults. I am going to leave out the Importance of Theory which is self-evident in all I have said. I am going to omit a "List of Strategies" since I am not an expert with adults. I am also going to leave out a "List of Values" and reserve that for Section IV.

That leaves us with eleven points which I will organize into three groupings: 1) Developmental, 2) Community, and 3) Analysis of the teacher-learner interaction.

Developmental Aspects

The points here are familiar because I have emphasized the developmental approach so often. These points in successful values education are:

The teacher understands the learner
The teacher teaches the whole person
The teacher teaches to developmental level

For the moment, I want to focus on teaching the whole person in adult education. Leon McKenzie refutes the conventional belief that "the religious educator of adults should not be concerned with human development viewed as a whole but only with those aspects of human development that are explicitly religious."[37] McKenzie believes that religion permeates all aspects of adult life. When we separate the sacred from the profane, we artificially eliminate opportunities for meaningful learning. "Religion is coextensive with life. The so-called secular experiences are pregnant with the possibility of religious meaning."[38]

Knowledge of development, what little we have of it at the adult level, can help us understand the whole learner and challenge that learner at his/her developmental level.

Community

The two aspects here are 1) the importance the family and 2) the development of community. I am suggesting that these two aspects are merged in adult education. In early childhood the two aspects are merged because the preschoolers family *is* the primary community. Later in development the child and teenager have two communities at least. Family as community continues, but school, peer group, church, and work group compete as other communities. The family will influence a learner throughout life, probably with diminishing returns for the adult learner as a primary support group. I am suggesting that adults in religious education who are struggling with religious values, need an intimate support group which we have called a community. Here is a challenge for the adult religious educator—whatever your group of adults (formal or informal), pay attention to building a community, a family of adults coadventuring in learning.

Analysis of the Teacher-Learner Interaction

There are seven points in this category which are clues to successful values education. First, I will list these points to help jog your memory.

1. Education is intentional
2. Education should be open-ended
3. Teachers are facilitators
4. Teachers arrange the learner's environment
5. An action-reflection model is involved
6. Teachers must be devoted to a long-term process
7. Teachers are in need of teacher training

Now I would like to comment on these points as I see them applying to adult religious education in values. I do not have much to add to "education is intentional." We must admit that unintentional education happens at random, particularly, perhaps, with adult learners. Adult learners have a wider experience base from which to continue learning, especially if they are self-motivated learners. My only suggestion here is to include your adults in planning educational objectives. Decide with them, not for them, what your group will learn.

A few, but not many adults will sit still for inculcation. An authoritarian approach may be easier for you. But I predict low attendance. Religious education particularly in values must be open-ended. Your values must take second place to the formation of each adult's own values.

You can but facilitate. You can but arrange your learner's environment to stimulate them to grow, each in her/his own way. Yes, you can indoctrinate a passive few. But adult education practice in this mode is not what I espouse. A full-blooded adult (or adolescent, for that matter) will revolt. My experience has been that whereas children will faithfully follow instructions in a testing situation, adults will follow only those instructions they care to follow.[39] I extrapolate to the learning situation in adult education. Adults should never be treated like children. Our inaccurate developmental knowledge of adults at least indicates that adults, however immature, are not children.

There are three more points not yet covered. As applied to successful values education they follow quite naturally although they may not seem very relevant to the teacher-learner interaction. However, I think they are. The first has to do with using the action-reflection model of learning. I would submit that one of the differences between childhood learning and adult learning has to do with relevance. We expect children to learn "things" which have no relevance to their lives in the belief that later on the knowledge will be good for them. Adults will not stand still for this rationale. Their motivation for learning is help for their immediate situation. If they need a skill—they learn a skill. Harking back to McKenzie, if they need to learn how to balance a budget (or how to grow green beans)—they learn how to balance a budget (or grow green beans). Budget balancing and growing green beans enhance their religious growth because they choose to reflect on such learning. Their best bet for such relevant learning is reflected in an action-reflection model of learning.

The next point is "devotion to a long-term process," at the adult level. I do not have much to add to Levinson or other explorers in adult development. But the suggestion from the research so far is that adult transitions are as long if not longer than we have seen in infancy, preschool, elementary school, early adolescence, or youth. The key phrase is "if not longer" for adults. Certainly, values education as applied to adults is a long-term process.

The last point I wish to make on values education for adults has to do with the extreme importance of trained teachers. I would go further than this and promote a matching, by developmental stage, between teacher and adult learner. A concrete thinking, conventional role taking and conformist teacher can hardly be expected to facilitate an adult learner toward abstract thinking, autonomous interdependence in role taking or autonomy in ego-development. A teacher who lacks self-actualizing experiences may be unable to challenge other adults to peak experiences.

Thus, adult religious educators must be chosen with

care and thoroughly trained to do a sensitive job in education with our sometimes mysterious adult learners.

This concludes our Maypole Dance and the Golden Braid of nine developmental theories. Before entering the final section of this book, a brief review and preview may be helpful.

Review and Preview

In Section I I introduced the subject of values. I tried to give a comprehensive evaluation of what values are both from the religious educators' perspective and from the secular psychologists' point of view. I did give some religious educators' lists of religious values. However, at that point I went no further than to choose, for the time being, the values of faith, hope, and love.

We next explored how to teach values in Section II. I gave you religious educators' strategies, and I gave you secular educators' strategies. We compared the two and found similarities which I made into a list of fourteen aspects for teaching values. A number of these fourteen aspects had to do with knowledge of development.

This section exposed you to nine developmental theories and their implications for religious education across the life cycle. For each of the developmental theories I tried to illustrate meanings for values education at the various age levels. I also tried to continue illustrating the fourteen so-called aspects for successfully teaching values.

I see two weaknesses in my progression thus far. At least, these are two areas with which I am uncomfortable at this point. The two areas are related and have to do with the question, what are Christian values? In the first place, I rather cavalierly gave you faith, hope, and love. I myself am convinced of the value of faith, hope, and love. Yet I ask myself are these *Christian* values? In the second place, while I gave you Christian lists from Miller, Kleinig, and Westerhoff, I did not resolve the differences. The question still remains—what are Christian values? A secondary question is, given a set of Christian values, what are the implications for religious education across the life cycle? Section IV is an exploratory answer, at this time and place, to those two questions. No book on teaching Christian values would be complete without some sort of answer.

Chapter 10 Notes and References

1. I am not the only religious educator who would use developmental knowledge. I have mentioned before such religious educators as Iris Cully, John Peatling, and Mary Wilcox, among others.

2. Merton P. Strommen, Milo L. Brekke, Ralph C. Underwager, and Arthur L. Johnson, *A Study of Generations* (Minneapolis: Augsburg Publishing House, 1972).

3. Ibid., p. 258.

4. Daniel J. Levinson, *The Seasons of a Man's Life* (New York: Ballantine Books, 1978).

5. Ibid., p. 20.

6. Naomi Golan, *Passing Through Transitions* (New York: The Free Press, 1981).

7. Ibid., chapter 3.

8. Robert J. Havighurst, *Human Development and Education* (London: Longmans Green, 1953).

9. Ronald Goldman, *Readiness for Religion* (London: Routledge and Kegan Paul, 1965).

10. Lucie W. Barber, *The Religious Education of Preschool Children* (Birmingham, Ala.: Religious Education Press, 1981).

11. Ibid., chapter 8.

12. Goldman, *Readiness for Religion,* pp. 47–48.

13. Ibid., chapter 7.

14. See James E. Loder, *The Transforming Moment* (San Francisco: Harper & Row, 1981), pp. 125–128 for an overview.

15. See Robert F. Peck and Robert J. Havighurst, *The Psychology of Character Development* (New York: John Wiley and Sons, 1960).

16. Erik H. Erikson, *Identity and the Life Cycle* (New York: W. W. Norton and Company, 1980).

17. The effect of teacher's level of development in moral judgment on learners' progress is well discussed by Ralph L. Mosher in "A Democratic High School: Damn It, Your Feet are Always in the Water," in *Value Development . . . As the Aim of Education* (Schenectady, N.Y.: Character Research Press, 1978).

18. Robert T. Gribbon, *When People Seek the Church* (Washington, D.C.: The Albin Institute, Inc., 1983).

19. Loder, *The Transforming Movement,* p. 38.

20. Ibid., p. 29.

21. Ibid., p. 31.

22. Ibid., p. 32.

23. Ibid.

24. Ibid., p. 33.

25. Ibid.

26. Ibid., p. 34.

27. Ibid., chapter 3.

28. Ibid., p. 92.

29. Jane Loevinger, *Ego Development* (San Francisco: Jossey-Bass Publications, 1980), p. 26.

30. Lawrence Kohlberg, "Educating for a Just Society: An Updated and Revised Statement," in *Moral Development, Moral Education and Kohlberg,* ed. Brenda Munsey (Birmingham, Ala.: Religious Education Press, 1980).

31. James W. Fowler, *Stages of Faith* (San Francisco: Harper & Row, 1981), chapter 21.

32. Jean Piaget, *Biology and Knowledge* (Chicago: University of Chicago Press, 1971).

33. Carol Gilligan and John Michael Murphy, "Development from Adolescence to Adulthood," in *Intellectual Development Beyond Childhood,* ed. Deanna Kuhn (San Francisco: Jossey-Bass, Inc., Publishers, 1979).

33. Ibid.

34. See chapter 4 of this book.

35. Ibid.

36. Ibid.

37. Leon McKenzie, *The Religious Education of Adults* (Birmingham, Ala.: Religious Education Press, 1982), p. 3.

38. Ibid., p. 8.

39. My experience consists in part of eighteen years of sending out questionnaires to children and adults. In the demographic sections, children answer every item without question. Adults simply do not.

SECTION IV

Seven Christian Values

CHAPTER 11

Another Maypole Dance

As we looked at nine theories in Section III we saw that each theory represented a progression from simple to complex on a continuum of maturity. An immature, newborn infant is simple compared to a complex, mature adult. Now I want to introduce one last theory which is so complex that I want to only introduce it. This is the Group Model of Integrated Personality.[1] First a few remarks about the Group Model.

1. The Group is a mathematical group (not a social group).[2]
2. The Group is very complex. Nonetheless, the model provides order in that the elements belonging to the Group follow mathematical rules when elements interact.[3]
3. I have worked with the Group Model for ten years and have found it extremely valuable for generating testable hypotheses.[4]

4. The Group Model represents healthy, integrated personality—the whole learner, if you will.[5]

I will be introducing the elements in the Group Model
shortly. A brief explanation of the origin of the elements is
in order. The Union College Character Research Project
was in the business of teaching values for thirty-five years.
The values came from the beatitudes in the Sermon on the
Mount. Toward the end of his career Ernest M. Ligon, the
founder of the Project, wanted to sum up his research in
character development. The initial elements in the Group
represented his ideas from the Project's experiences in
teaching values.[6] Ligon must also be credited with the insight that elements interact according to the mathematics
of a Group. Ligon was unable to finish the work. John
Peatling and, later, David Tiedeman continued and were
able to publish a book, *Designing Self,* which is a full description of the Group Model.[7]

Thus the Group Model is grounded in Christian values.
I posit that the interactions between elements can be stated
in value terms. Thus, I propose to introduce you to the
elements and their interactions by way of another Maypole
Dance. Finally, I propose to give you value statements dictated by the Group Model. These statements give us a list
of Christian values for religious education.

Only two strands start at the top of the pole (see Figure 3).
Yet there are sixteen strands at the bottom. Let the dance
begin. Whatever direction the sixteen dancers go, those two
top strands are going to interrelate. Not only the two top
strands but the next four, the next eight and the final sixteen strands are going to interrelate. It would be fascinating
to actually see this Maypole Dance. It might be more com-

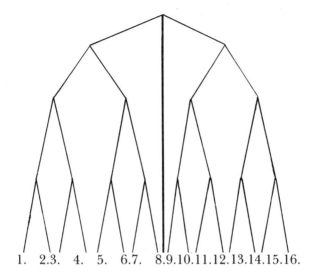

FIGURE 3.   THE GROUP MODEL MAYPOLE

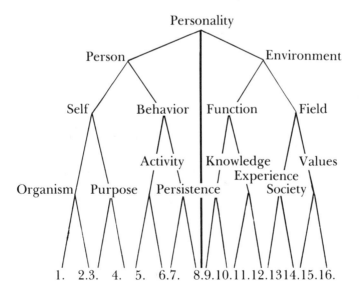

FIGURE 4.   NAMES OF ELEMENTS (STRANDS) IN THE GROUP
MODEL MAYPOLE.[8]

plicated than the most dazzling square dance with its multiple dance steps.

I do not propose to teach you all of the dance steps. I propose only to take from that odd-looking maypole the dance steps that will be of most use to you. In order for you to make any sense of the dance of religious education, I will introduce you to the names of the strands. See Figure 4.

The Sixteen Dancers

1. Uniqueness
   It is "a philosophically posited attribute that is presumed to be present from the moment of conception." Since it is an "it," let us set it on the sidelines for our dance.
2. Endowments
   This dancer is "what an individual can, in fact, do at any given moment."
3. Self-Image
   This dancer is "the picture an individual has of himself or herself as a total personality."
4. Vision
   This dancer is "an individually held, pervasive, goal specific self-related intention."
5. Action is "overt or observable behavior (i.e., activity) including a 'willingness' to engage in such behavior."
6. Growth is the "degree to which a complex, genetically controlled range of possibilities is approximated."

7. Courage is "basically, individual persistence."
8. Judgment
    This dancer wears quite a costume—"the level of complexity of information one regards as relevant and/or 'necessary' when called upon to choose one from among several 'evident' courses of action."

There you have the eight dancers on the Person side of the Maypole. Now we will look at the eight dancers on the Environment side.

9. Decision Making
    This "is basically (and initially) the action of choosing."
10. Learning
    This dancer "is, basically, the ability to acquire and use 'new' information and/or skills."
11. Home Resources
    Home Resources "are what an individual perceives to be available to him or her as a 'resource' in his or her 'home.'"
12. Roles
    The costume on this dancer is "complex behavioral patterns that are relatively consistent across considerable periods of time."
13. Measures of Character
    That seems an odd name for a dancer. It is "one's basic perceptions of one's own placement within the personally known World."
14. World
    "The societal environment outside the 'narrow' limits of one's home (or surrogate home) and immediate family"

15. Evaluation
"A set of available and used skills for comparing actuality to known and accepted standards."

16. Philosophy
This is the sixteenth dancer and the one who will lead the dance. She is "a complex, organized system of thinking about principles and values, and about their relationship to experiential 'reality.'"

There are our sixteen dancers. The name of the dance is "Religious Education." We will lead off the dance with dancer sixteen, Philosophy, because she is the one who most closely resembles religion. But the dance of religious education will involve all the other dancers. In order to keep track of the dancers, let us put signs on each. On the signs will be the first letter or facsimile of each dancer's name. Thus if I identify a dance step as EoX → P, you will know that Endowments and Evaluation are dancing together for Philosophy.

The Dance Steps

The Maypole makes it look as though the dance, religious education, is going to be very complicated. Lo and behold, there are only seven dance steps! Here they are:

$$EoX \rightarrow P$$
$$SoW \rightarrow P$$
$$VoM \rightarrow P$$
$$AoR \rightarrow P$$
$$GoH \rightarrow P$$
$$CoL \rightarrow P$$

JoD → P

I could tell you that all those strands operate according to the properties of an abelian group (that is a mathematical group). I could also point out that the theory for the Group Model posits a high degree of orderliness for Personality. However, let us return to the dance.

I am going to reorder the dance steps around Philosophy. She is the one getting all the attention.

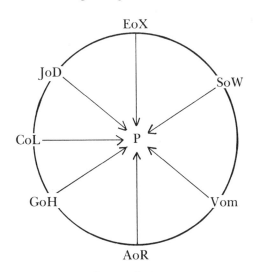

FIGURE 5.   THE SEVEN INTERACTIONS IN THE GROUP MODEL WHICH RESULT IN THE ELEMENT, PHILOSOPHY

Forget the title for Figure 5 for the time being. The figure shows you the dance. One last task for me to do is to find titles for the seven dance steps. These are my present titles (I reserve the right to change them in the future as my knowledge increases).

EoX — P:Perceiving One's Talents Objectively
SoW — P:Self-Acceptance
VoM — P:Intentional Vocation
AoR — P:Purposeful Behavior
GoH — P:Spiritual Guidance
CoL — P:Courage with Learning
JoD — P:Wise Decision Making

Only the most mature dancers can dance those steps. My sixteen dancers are described by the stage titles on pages 158–159 for people in their 50s. The dance steps together represent The Potential of Religious Education. They are ultimate goals for values education. They are values for religious education.

First I want to indicate how I named the dance steps. You have been briefly introduced to the sixteen dancers. I have been personal friends with those dancers for over ten years. I know their dance troupe intimately. I know their union rules for how they will dance. Thus I did not pull the titles for the dance steps out of the blue. Take E.X—as an example. I know their parents, their grandparents, their great grand parents and their great, great grand-parent. Their great, great grandparent is called Person-ality. Thus I had a good deal to go on in naming the Endowments and Evaluation dance step.

The Group Model of Personality

Now, we must go from the fun of a dance as modeled by a mathematical group of personality elements to the im-plications for values education. I named the dance steps or the interactions leading to P (philosophy). Out of the pos-sible sixteen elements, I chose P as the element for the whole learner which best represents the complexities of religious education. Furthermore, I am positing that the seven interactions for P are useful clues in naming seven values for Christians which are inclusive for a whole learner.

Now I want to take the seven Christian values, inspect them in light of developmental theories and then begin to identify each value with the religious education literature. At first my terminology may seem strange. Perhaps I can modify the strangeness.

One final word. In this chapter, I will only be talking about the seven Christian values as they might apply to a most *mature* Christian. I decline to fully associate a most mature Christian at a level 6 in developmental theories. I do not want to make the "fallacy of the Stage 6s." However, Stage 6s have a great deal to do with what I want to say because from a humanitarian point of view Stage 6s describe our far reaches of knowledge even if they are incomplete descriptions.

Perceiving Talents Objectively

When the element Endowments interacts with the element Evaluation the result is part of one's Philosophy. The combination of Endowments and Evaluation suggest the value of "Perceiving Talents Objectively." Evaluation skills help us toward objectivity. We can be objective about our Endowments.

Really mature religious persons can transcend any ego-defensiveness about their skills, inherited or learned. The objectivity which self-actualization makes possible gives the persons a quality of appreciating the reality of their strengths and weaknesses. They are in tune, therefore, with a higher reality which is God's plan. They can perceive their talents in relation to God's plan.

"In each of us the Spirit is manifested in one particular way, for some useful purpose. One man, through the Spirit, has the gift of wise speech, while another, by the power of the same spirit, can put the deepest knowledge into words. Another, by the same Spirit, is granted faith; another, by the one Spirit, gifts of healing, and another miraculous powers; another has the gift of prophecy; and another ability to distinguish true spirits from false; yet another has the gift of ecstatic utterance of different kinds, and another the ability to interpret it."[9] As we are objective about our endowments so can we find our way to best serve.

For religious educators, perhaps the term, gifts, instead of talents makes more sense. Sara Little, reporting on a colloquium on the future of educational ministry, noted, "The education we see emerging is one that will make use of the gifts given to people."[10] A mature Christian, then, must be realistic about such bestowed gifts. And that is what "Perceiving Talents Objectively" is all about.

Self-Acceptance

When the element Self-Image interacts with the element World the result is part of one's Philosophy. The combination of Self-Image and World suggest the value of Self-Acceptance. We place ourselves in our world or universe and are able to accept ourselves as part of that "out there."

Perry's commitment in relativism is particularly relevant here as are Loevinger's Stage 6 and Maslow's Self-Actualization. Not only are mature persons able to deal with complexities, they can develop the self-confidence to thrive in such an environment. They can solve life's problems with integrity as Erikson might put it.[11]

"Love your neighbor as yourself" is the second great commandment. We start life as egocentrics. The chain of progression is: love self → love others → love God.

Randolph Crump Miller completes the cycle. "Because God is love and loves us, we are struck with the realization of our own worth as creatures of God."[12] We can love self because God loves us.

In *Religious Conversion and Personal Identity,* V. Bailey Gillespie relates conversion and self-identity.[13] In conversion we find our identity and can accept ourselves.

Intentional Vocation

When the element Vision interacts with the element Measures of Character, the result is part of one's Philosophy. The combination of Vision and Measures of Character ("one's basic perceptions of one's own placement within the personally know World") suggests the value of Intentional Vocation.

First, as I have done before, I want to clarify my meaning from the point of view of the nine theories I presented in Section 3. When we think of a religiously mature adult, we encounter an abstract thinker, committed in relativism, who knows being rather than just becoming, who transcends and integrates. Also, a religiously mature adult wills her/his life in order to approximate the will of God. This, it seems to me, has to do with an intentional vocation.

I am using the term vocation in the religious sense. Vocation is a calling from God: "As God has called you, live up to your calling."[14] I am aware from my training in counseling and guidance that there is confusion about the terms vocation and career. For example, Donald Super gave us a theory of vocational development in the 1950s.[15] In practice, vocational education has been related to job training. A different atmosphere invaded the 1970s and is with us today. The term, vocation, is being replaced by the term, career.

I am taking the term career as enunciated by David V. Tiedeman[16] as representing what I mean by "Intentional Vocation." Tiedeman, as director of the National Institute for Advancement in Career Education, sees career as living out a life for which the person is responsible. This emphasis on responsibility for one's life (one's work vocationally and avocationally) is what I am trying to get at by "Intentional Vocation."

Mature Christians intend their lives to mean something in God's plan for us. We can plan an intentional response to God's call to us. In James Fowler's description of Stage 6, Universalizing Faith, he uses slightly different language. However, attend to his words, "Seen in the light of this vision the human vocation—and it must be understood as a universal human vocation—is to live in anticipation of the coming reign of God. The human vocation is to lean into God's promised future for us and for all being. It is to be part of the reconciling, redeeming, and restoring work that goes on wherever the Kingdom of God is breaking in."[17]

Purposeful Behavior

When the element Action interacts with the element Roles the result is part of one's Philosophy. The combination of Action and Roles suggests the value of "Purposeful Behavior."

Of the nine theories described in Section III, perhaps Piaget's affectivity stages are most useful for the action and roles interaction. Piaget proposes *will* starting at Stage 5. Then, in his description of Stage 6, Idealistic Feelings, he says a person "assigns himself a role and goals in social life." The willfulness of assigning oneself a role and goals describes "Purposeful Behavior." A mature Christian can decide the roles and behavior she/he will live. In Maslow's terms these behaviors will be *being* behaviors for self-actualization. In Loevinger's terms such behaviors will be integrated within the total complex ego. Career decisions, in Tiedeman's terms, will be integrated with respect to responsibility for self and others.

In Scripture, the term "acts" is likely to replace action or behavior. "Even a child makes himself known by his acts, whether what he does is pure and right."[18] At the adult level James writes, "But he who looks into the perfect law, the law of liberty, and perseveres, being no hearer that forgets but a doer that acts, he shall be blessed in his doing."[19]

"Fruits" is another term that replaces action or behavior. Matthew in discussing false prophets quotes Jesus as saying, "Thus you will know them by their fruits."[20] Finally, the term "deed" is found. "And whatever you do, in word or deed, do everything in the name of the Lord Jesus, giving thanks to God the Father through him."[21] For a Christian, purposeful behavior is behaving in the name of Christ in order to do the will of God.

Gillespie in *Religious Conversion and Personal Identity* has a good deal to say about roles. His interest is in role experimentation that is part of seeking an identity. Adolescents try out various roles seeking roles that fit. A religious conversion based on a negative identity is not desirable. Religious educators must challenge youth to try out positive roles. Religious conversion should be freely chosen based on a positive identity. "Purposeful Behavior" at the mature level, then becomes purposefully choosing roles for one's behavior, roles which glorify God.

Westerhoff speaks more directly about adults and roles and action. Within an affirming community "we need: (a) To be provided with experiences foundational to moral decision making and be exposed to role models of the Christian life; (b) to be given opportunities to apply Christian faith to individual and social life; (c) to be enabled to act and reflect faithfully and responsibly in our daily individual and corporate lives, to the end that God's kingdom comes and God's will is done."[22]

Spiritual Guidance

When the element Growth interacts with the element Home Resources the result is part of one's Philosophy. The combination of Growth and Home Resources suggest the value of "Spiritual Guidance." Growth, it will be recalled, is "the degree to which a complex, genetically controlled range of possibilities is approximated." Home Resources "are what an individual perceives to be available to him or her as a 'resource' in his or her 'home.'"

This particular interaction is important to guidance counselors and therapists. Growth is related to potential. Achieving potential for clients is a goal for guidance counselors who become Home Resources when they are able to establish a helping relationship with clients. Adolescents and adults can well perceive their counselors or therapists as intimate, personal resources, a kind of home base.

In fact, therapy may help adults to integration of ego, and/or to self-actualization, and/or commitment in relativism. With or without help, GoH—P is a possibility for mature adults. Such maturity is called integrity in Erikson's language.[23] However, a religiously mature person needs to question the meaning of Home Resources. Certainly preschool children look to parents for guidance. Young adults look to mentors or therapists for guidance. Mature, religious adults who are autonomous and have a strong identity have a spiritual resource available to them. Let us look next at how Scripture deals with the spiritual guidance interaction of Growth and Home Resources.

My concordance led me to the terms Grow(s), Guide, and Counselor as helpful. "Now the boy Samuel continued to grow both in stature and in favor with the Lord and with men."[24] This reminds us of, "And Jesus increased in wisdom and in stature and favor with God and man."[25] These quotes suggest growth toward potential. But exactly how are we to grow towards potential? "Rather, speaking the truth in love, we are to grow up in every way into him who is the head, into Christ, from whom the whole body, joined and knit together by every joint with which it is supplied, when each part is working properly, makes bodily growth and upbuilds itself in love."[26] "But grow in the grace and knowledge of our Lord and Savior Jesus Christ."[27]

The terms Guide and Counselor suggest Home Resources. The term Guide is an Old Testament word for God. "Yea, thou art my rock and my fortress; for thy name's sake lead me and guide me, take me out of the net which is hidden for me, for thou art my refuge."[28] "That this is God, our God for ever and ever. He will be our guide for ever."[29] "Thou does guide me with thy counsel, and afterward thou wilt receive me to glory."[30]

Finally, the term Counselor for our purposes is found in both Old and New Testaments, but both refer to Jesus and the Holy Spirit. "For to us a child is born, to us a son is given; and the government will be upon his shoulder, and his name will be called 'Wonderful Counselor, Mighty God, Everlasting Father, Prince of Peace'."[31] "But the Counselor, the Holy Spirit, whom the Father will send in my name, he will teach you all things, and bring to your remembrance all that I have said to you."[32]

The Scriptures I have chosen suggest a "Spiritual Guidance." The Scriptures I have not chosen suggest a negative influence of the devil, false prophets, and sin. Let us turn to contemporary religious education on the spiritual guidance interaction.

I believe that Fowler is talking about growth toward potential in his description of his Stage 6, Universalizing Faith. "Stage 6 is exceedingly rare. The persons best described by it have generated faith compositions in which their felt sense of an ultimate environment is inclusive of all being. They have become incarnators and actualizers of the spirit of an inclusive and fulfilled human community."[33] Stage 6 describes Fowler's most mature faithing persons. These persons are lured by the coming of the Kingdom of God, by the power of the future.[34] We must infer guidance here.

Miller uses quite different language. He speaks of opening ourselves to an appreciation of values as a way to grow. God is the source of values. One way to know God and his works is through values. "The educational implications . . . are obvious. Good education will tap the potentialities in each learner. Teachers will seek to discover the direction in which a student should be led and provide the stimulation to unleash the opportunities for development. Values will be presented as a way of stirring the imagination and of inspiring new aspirations."[35]

But what does Miller have to say about guidance. "People, living in the finite perspective of history, can align themselves with the processes which God has set in action, and in so doing they can *approximate* God's will."[36] They must be alert to such processes "through every tool at their command." Thus, "Human beings have access to the transforming and energizing presence of God as a means for achieving values."[37] Again, we are called on to infer guidance.

In the matter of guidance, I suspect most religious educators would consider prayer. "Prayer is the discipline of paying attention to what, by our repentance, God gives to us."[38] Dykstra warns us that paying attention is a hard discipline. But our attentiveness to God rather than ourselves "provides the energy and light we need."[39] Prayer can provide "Spiritual Guidance" for mature Christians.

Courage with Learning

As an illustration of what I mean by "Courage with Learning," I will use as an example an interview of a minister with a search committee. The minister was asked about his personal prayer life. After prolonged thought, the minister answered that he joined in common prayers of worship, and beyond that his prayer life consisted of established, liturgical utterances that sustained him. He risked misunderstanding. He dared. The search committee recommended him because they saw that his honesty in courageous learning of God's will superseded theirs—and that's what they wanted in a minister. His whole life was a prayer.

To put the value of "Courage with Learning" into psychologists' terms, I can think immediately about Maslow's self-actualizers. If a self-actualizer related a peak experience, we would probably think her/him crazy. Yet, relate these experiences she/he must. When a person, a mature person, is integrated (in Loevinger's, Tiedeman's, or Erikson's terms), then, "Courage with Learning," it seems to me, is a must. Call it wisdom, but don't older adults who are mature owe it to younger generations to pass down to them accrued knowledge? It takes courage to do this, to be sure, but experienced persons can do this because religiously they *must.*

There is a story about Paul in Acts which I think illustrates "Courage with Learning." Paul was in difficulties with the Sadduces and Pharisees in Jerusalem. The Jews were planning to kill him. "The following night the Lord stood by him and said, 'Take courage, for as you have testified about me at Jerusalem, so you must bear witness also at Rome.'"[40] The Roman governor had Paul put in jail in Caesarea to protect him from the Jews. Finally, King Agrippa arrived in Caesarea. The governor, Festus, had Paul brought to the audience hall. There Paul testified about Jesus and told of the learning from his Damascus experience. "And as he thus made his defense, Festus said with a loud voice, 'Paul, you are mad; your great learning is turning you mad.' But Paul said, 'I am not mad, most excellent Festus, but I am speaking the sober truth.'"[41] Paul continued to witness, even trying to convert King Agrippa and the rest of the assembled court. His courage and persistence impressed the court and Paul was allowed to begin his perilous voyage to Rome where he continued preaching and teaching.

As for religious educators, I believe everyone whom I have already cited in this book is an example of "Courage with Learning." In order to write a book, a great deal of learning is necessary which the author then has the courage to share with readers.

There is one final value from the Group Model which we will inspect next.

Wise Decision Making

When the element Judgment interacts with the element Decision Making, the result is a part of one's Philosophy. The combination of Judgment and Decision Making suggests the value of "Wise Decision Making."

You will recall that Judgment is "the level of complexity of information one regards as relevant and/or 'necessary' when called upon to choose one from among several 'evident' courses of action." Decision making is "the action of choosing." Wise decisions are decisions based on judgment where the level of complexity of information is high.

Tiedeman's Stage of Integration in career decision making is a good example. After Induction and Reformation the wise decision to Integrate is based on complex information about Self and co-workers. The decision is responsible to both Self and others. Loevinger's most mature level of ego development, Integration, occurs in those persons able to deal with great complexities. This is true for Perry's Commitment in Relativism and Maslow's Self-Actualization. Dealing with complexities presupposes Peatling's Very Abstract stage in cognition.

Before turning to Scripture and to religious educators, I would like to interject some feelings or intuitions I have about Judgment. We have treated that element quite cold-bloodedly so far. The Group Model presents Judgment as the multiplication of Endowments, Self, and Action on the Person side of the Model. In other words, Judgment is very personal. However, all the interactions for Philosophy are between a Person element and an Environment element. And Philosophy is the multiplication of Endowments, Self, Action, and Decision Making. Thus, I imagine that Judgment is heavily loaded with one's personal values.

"Inspired decisions are on the lips of a king; his mouth does not sin in judgment."[42] Does the writer of Proverbs mean the motivation of personal values in inspired decisions or something more? John quotes Jesus as saying, "I can do nothing on my own authority; as I hear, I judge and my judgment is just, because I seek not my own will but the will of him who sent me."[43] Seeking God's will calls for a high level of complexity of information. John further prays "that your faith might not rest in the wisdom of men but in the power of God."[44]

Clearly, religious educators think in terms of God's will in "Wise Decision Making." This is an addition to humanists' interpretation of the Judgment and Decision Making interaction. But seeking God's will for a mature Christian is no easy matter. "We do it in a much more complex and confusing world, one that includes the future and the past as well as the present, the abstract as well as the concrete, the facticity of existence as known through reflection as well as through immediate experience."[45] Since the information that mature persons deal with in making judgments is so complex, most religious educators in mainline denominations, including the Roman Catholics, insist on the chooser's freedom. *Religious Education, Catechesis, and Freedom,* by Kenneth R. Barker, explicates a freedom position.[46]

Another voice says, "Liberation becomes a possibility only when freedom can be established as a means. Process thought builds on the principles of relativity and indeterminacy and allows for chance and novelty as essential in the process of becoming and perishing. Thus, metaphysically, there is room for a genuine freedom as human beings move from where they are to where they can envision themselves as being, guided by goals which they are capable of developing and implementing."[47]

In speaking about authority in religious education, Miller goes on to say, "Freedom is exemption from *arbitrary* authority or necessity in thought and action. It is a way of acknowledging authority or refusing to acknowledge it."[48] "Authority in education, then, is never the denial of the student's freedom to think; it never insists upon agreement; it depends on its own merits to persuade and is open to response from the learner."[49]

Concluding Remarks

I have introduced you to Group Theory which led me to proclaim seven Christian values for the whole learner who is a mature, religious person. These values were: 1) Perceiving Talents Objectively, 2) Self-Acceptance, 3) Intentional Vocation, 4) Purposeful Behavior, 5) Spiritual Guidance, 6) Courage with Learning, 7) Wise Decision Making. Certainly you have noted that these seven values are not isolated categories. They appear to complement each other. For example, it is easier to "Perceive Talents Ojbectively" if one has "Self Acceptance." Or clues to "Intentional Vocation" are found in "Purposeful Behavior," or vice versa. "Wise Decision Making" is helped by "Spiritual Guidance." I could go on, but the point is that the model dictates the interrelationship between interactions. Philosophy is made up of the seven interactions, or, to put it another way, the seven interactions represent the whole of Philosophy.[50] Philosophy, you will recall is "a complex, organized system of thinking about principles and values, and about their relationship to experiential 'reality.'"[51] The definition given here sums up what I believe are ultimate goals of religious education if the term thinking is accepted in the widest sense. By widest sense for thinking, I refer to my Golden Braid—affective plus cognitive thinking, interpersonal perspective taking, idealistic feelings, and integration of all forms of thinking plus self-actualization.

That is all very well when considering ultimate goals for religious education in values. In the following and last chapter, I would like to present a system of religious education based on the seven interactions for Philosophy in the Group Model. This approach to religious education, which combines developmental theories with a new theory, the Group Model of Personality Integration, may give you insights because the approach has not been taken before.

Chapter 11 Notes and References

1. Lucie W. Barber and John H. Peatling, "A Statement About a Model of Personality," Schenectady, N.Y. (Unpublished

Ms.), 1974. Footnotes 2, 3, 4 and 5 come from this paper and from Dr. Peatling's address at the 1974 American Personnel and Guidance Association's Annual Convention in New Orleans.

2. The Group Model is an abelian group which is an hierarchial structure. We work with 5 levels at the present time.

3. At each level the elements interact. The elements themselves are the Cartesian products of an Identity element and a n-1 generator elements. Each element is its own inverse. Within the constraints of this set of mathematical rules, the interaction of two elements is a simple algebraic multiplication.

4. *The Barber Scales of Self Regard: Preschool* were based on the seven interactions for Self-Image and form the basis for *Realistic Parenting* (St. Meinard, Ind.: Abbey Press, 1980).

5. At the most general level, there is one element, Personality. The next level has two elements, Person and Environment, which constitute Personality. The next level has four elements, two of which constitute Person and two of which constitute Environment. The next level has eight elements. The fifth level has sixteen elements which constitute level 4 elements. Thus the model represents the whole of personality.

6. Ernest M. Ligon, "A Map for Character Development: Mathematical Group Theory," *Character Potential: A Record of Research,* 5 (1–2) (July 1970).

7. John H. Peatling and David V. Tiedeman, *Career Development: Designing Self* (Muncie, Ind.: Accelerated Development, 1977). The quoted definitions of the Group Model elements (dancers) come from this book, pp. 114–119.

8. The names of the elements in Figure 4 represent the hierarchial levels 1, 2, 3 and 4. The numbers at the bottom of Figure 4 are the elements in level 5. See the definitions of the dancers.

9. 1 Corinthians 12:7–10. The New English Bible.

10. Sara Little, "Reflections on What Happened: The Future of Educational Ministry," *Religious Education* (July-August, 1978).

11. Erik H. Erikson, *Identity, Youth, and Crisis* (New York: W. W. Norton and Company, 1968).

12. Randolph Crump Miller, *The Theory of Christian Education Practice* (Birmingham, Ala.: Religious Education Press, 1980), p. 194.

13. V. Bailey Gillespie, *Religious Conversion and Personal Identity* (Birmingham, Ala.: Religious Education Press, 1979).

14. Ephesians 4:1 RSV.

15. Donald E. Super, *Psychology of Careers* (New York: Macmillan, 1957).

16. David V. Tiedeman, "The Self-Constructionist Alternative to Today's Develop or Wither Career Crisis at Mid-Life," and "Discerning 'I' Power in the Developmental Paradigm at Mid-Life," *Character Potential: A Record of Research* 8 (3) (February, 1978).

17. James W. Fowler, *Stages of Faith* (San Francisco: Harper & Row, 1981), p. 210.

18. Proverbs 20:11, RSV.

19. James 1:25, RSV.

20. Matthew 7:20, RSV.

21. Colossians 3:17, RSV.

22. John H. Westerhoff, III, *Will Our Children Have Faith?* (New York: Seabury, 1976), p. 108. See also John H. Westerhoff III and Gwen Kennedy Neville, *Generation to Generation* (Philadelphia: United Church Press, 1974), chapter 9, "Reshaping Adults."

23. Erik H. Erikson, *Identity and the Life Cycle* (New York: W. W. Norton and Company, 1980).

24. 1 Samuel 2:26, RSV.

25. Luke 2:52, RSV.

26. Ephesians 4:15, RSV.

27. 2 Peter 3:18, RSV.

28. Psalms 31:3, RSV.

29. Ibid., 46:14, RSV.

30. Ibid., 73:24, RSV.

31. Isaiah 9:6, RSV.

32. John 14:26, RSV.

33. Fowler, *Stages of Faith*, p. 200.

34. Ibid., pp. 210–211.

35. Miller, *The Theory of Christian Education Practice*, p. 131.

36. Ibid., p. 142.

37. Ibid., pp. 143–144.

38. Craig Dykstra, *Vision and Character* (New York: Paulist Press, 1981), p. 95).

39. Ibid., p. 98.

40. Acts 23:11, RSV.

41. Acts 26:24, 25, RSV.

42. Proverbs 16:10, RSV.

43. John 5:30, RSV.

44. 1 Corinthians 2:5, RSV.

45. Dykstra, *Vision and Character*, p. 142.

46. Kenneth R. Barker, *Religious Education, Catechesis, and Freedom* (Birmingham, Ala.: Religious Education Press, 1981).

47. Miller, *The Theory of Christian Education Practice*, p. 38.

48. Ibid., p. 175.

49. Ibid., p. 176.

50. Actually, there are eight interactions which result in Philosophy. We have ommitted P.U—P because in all honesty, we have been unable to interpret the identity interaction adequately. The identity element in the Group Model is Uniqueness at level 5. At the very least each person's Philosophy is unique.

51. "Thinking about principles and values and about the relationship to experiential reality," is another clue to understanding the mature, religious person and our goals in religious education. How else do we seek to do God's will?

CHAPTER 12

An Educational System

I described seven Christian values in the previous chapter. Those descriptions applied to mature, religious persons. Assuming that mature, religious persons is the ultimate goal of religious education, what are our proximate goals for immature religious persons? What do we teach preschoolers, children, adolescents, and young adults? I am going to suggest a step-by-step, backward progression. If that sounds like a contradiction, bear with me.

Step 1. Start with mature, religious adults and let their values serve as ultimate goals. This is what we accomplished in chapter 11.

Step 2. Think about persons at the 16-28-year-old developmental level in relation to the mature adults in Step 1. How can the 16-28-year-olds approximate the mature adults? How can they be helped to grow and develop? When

you have answers to those questions, you can set learning objectives for 16-28-year-olds in religious education.

Step 3. Think about early adolescents (12-15-year-olds) in relation to 16-28-year-olds. How can they be helped to grow
and approximate the 16-28-year-olds: Set learning objectives for the early adolescents.

Step 4. Think about elementary school children (6-11-year-
olds) in relation to 12-15-year-olds. How can they be
helped to grow and approximate the early adolescents?
Set learning objectives for these children.

Step. 5. Finally, think about preschool children (2-5-year-olds)
in relation to 6-11-year-olds. How can they be helped to
grow and approximate the elementary school children?
Set learning objectives for preschool children.[1]

This is what I mean by a step by step, backward progression. This is what I will do in this chapter. We will progress
backward through the developmental levels discussing
learning objectives for each of the seven values. When we
get through, we will have a life cycle, educational system in
values education.

Perceiving Talents Objectively

Perceiving talents objectively is our ultimate goal for this
interaction from the Group Model. However, we do not
expect little children to be objective about their endowments. At each developmental level, the interaction will be
interpreted differently and can be given a title appropriate
to development at that level. What follows are my tentative

titles[2] for the EoX—P interaction in a step by step backward progression.

CHRISTIAN MATURITY	PERCEIVING TALENTS OBJECTIVELY
16–28 Years	Evaluating Contributions
12–15 Years	Learning Evaluation Skills
6–11 Years	Perceiving Talents of Self and Others
2–5 Years	Discovering Talents

Titles can be deceiving because they are often collapsed in scope and omit full meaning. Thus I want to briefly comment on each developmental level. In the meantime, return a moment to the list of titles above. Start at the bottom and read up. Notice the progression as development proceeds.

Christian Maturity

To summarize what was said about a mature Christian in chapter 11, a mature Christian can overcome ego-defensiveness and attain an objective perception of talents and how they can be used to serve God.

16-28 Years—Evaluating Contributions

How can late adolescents and young adults be helped toward "Perceiving Talents Objectively?" You will recall that autonomy is their battle. Their idealistic feelings, their esteem needs, their reformation in career makes transcendence that comes with self-actualization difficult.

Their religious education should include opportunities to view their talents objectively. The best way I know to facilitate viewing talents objectively is to let youth and adults get into the parish action. Let them find out what talents they have for the church barbecue, the arts fair, the Bible study group, the Sunday social hour, the church school, the vestry or hospital calling. Every parish has numerous opportunities for youth and adults to try out their talents. They will need help in "Evaluating their Talents Objectively."

12-15 Years—Learning Evaluation Skills

It is probably very difficult for early adolescents to perceive their talents objectively. They are caught up in puberty for one thing. These physical changes come at the same time as cognitive and affective changes occur. Self-protection in the peer group provides a buffer zone as all the new competencies unfold. Early adolescence is a magnificent developmental level. It is also difficult and confusing.

In relation to talent, I believe that there are two tasks for the religious educator working with early adolescents: 1) facilitating learners to fulfill their esteem needs by providing opportunities within the peer group for recognized accomplishments, and 2) helping learners with the skills for ordering complex data sets. These early adolescents need to experience their talents and they need skills to prepare themselves for eventually perceiving their talents objectively.

6-11 Years—Perceiving Talents of Self and Others

Elementary school children can only perceive their talents concretely and in relation only to the groups to which they belong (classroom, family, playground, etc.). They compare their competencies with those of others and can accept that others are more skilled than they are. However, each learner excels in some areas. The religious educator can assess the strengths and weaknesses of each learner and then encourage learners to concentrate on strengths as God's gift. This is a step along the way, an important step.

2-5 Years—Discovering Talents

I am going to leave the Preschool developmental level for the end of the chapter where we will discuss the Preschoolers across all the Group Model interactions in one section.

Self-Acceptance

Christian Maturity

Mature Christians can not only deal with the complexities of our world, they can also transcend the complexities and find a commitment in relativity. They can accept themselves because of God's love.

16-28 Years—Autonomy of Self in Society

How can religious educators help late teens and young adults approximate mature self-acceptance? We can help them value "Autonomy of Self in Society." The move toward true adulthood means a move from the school womb to the marketplace of the "real" world—not an easy transition. Their religious education should include educational objectives that lead toward finding their place in God's creation. I can think of projects in interrelationships and coping with complexities. Specific projects might be Preparation for Marriage or Parenting Training.

12-15 Years—Identity in Peer Group

How can religious educators help prepare early teenagers for "Autonomy of Self in Society"? They must first have a foundation of "Identity in Peer Group." These are years in a kind of buffer zone between childhood and adulthood. They need to identify with their peers after the dependence of childhood on parents and school. They need to build self-confidence before they can proceed with further independence in late adolescence. However, they also need challenges to their faith as their abstract thinking and idealistic feelings emerge. This is their first encounter with religion beyond childhood's concrete thinking. They can no longer be treated like or taught like children.

6-11 Years—Identity in School

The step toward mature "Self-Acceptance" that can be taken at this developmental level involves Self in concrete society. These children are just learning about the feelings of others and how to behave so that they are acceptable and accepted. They learn the rules. Early morality begins. They can feel guilt for wrongdoing. They still tend to submit to authority: parents, teachers, ministers, or priests. Yet some of the more mature begin to question the rules. If religious educators can appreciate development, they will not expect too much of elementary school children for this interaction of the Group Model.

2-5 Years—Self in Family and Play Group

Intentional Vocation

Christian Maturity

Mature Christians plan their careers as vocations (callings) to live their lives as though the kingdom of God is breaking in, in Fowler's terms. They must be responsible to themselves, others and God.

16-28 Years—Identity in the Career World

How can persons at this developmental level be helped toward an "Intentional Vocation" just described?

You and I understand vocation as a calling from God. We think of career as a calling. We do not equate it with the secular sense of a job whereby we can pay for the food on the table. Let us face it—most young adults must pay the rent or mortgage and put food on the table, meet car payments, loans on baby furniture, or loans for education.

Our young adults need help with an "Intentional Vocation." They must be helped to transcend the social pressures of wage earning vs. answering God's call and purposefully striving for an "Intentional Vocation."

12-15 Years—Beginning Abstraction of Life Goals.

It is common for early adolescents to fantasize about life goals. This is a step forward from childhood concreteness. They are not yet realistic in an adult sense. They are dreamers. This is fine. But they can be helped.

One of the most difficult things for people to realize is that they can have a say about what happens in their lives. Intentional vocation may be a concept beyond the understanding of most early adolescents. However, a step along the way is to provide them with experiences of running their own youth group, making things happen in their parish because of their own decisions, and choosing themselves what religious information they will learn.

6-11 Years—Concretizing Life Goals

What can religious educators do to prepare children for the idea of life goals and eventually for "Intentional Vocation?"

Career education in many schools today is a K - 12 involvement. That does not mean that elementary school children are taught to write resumes or how to interview for a job. However, they can be taught attitudes about work, they can be exposed to stories and people in many careers, and they can be guarded against sex-role stereotyping in careers. I believe the church can play a part here. Why cannot these children learn what it means to be a minister or priest in everyday life? Your career and the careers of people in your parish are other examples. At a concrete level, the idea of worker or helpers for God seems to me to be appropriate.

2-5 Years—Fantasizing Life Goals

Purposeful Behavior

Christian Maturity

Mature Christians choose to behave and live their lives for the purpose of doing God's will as best they can ascertain that will through Jesus Christ.

16-28 Years—Action for a Purpose

At this level of development young adults can handle multiplicity and relativism. They can think abstractly and feel about ideas. However, these new competencies come at a time in life when two tasks are all important: self-identity and establishment of oneself in the job market. In order to be independent, youth must choose roles for earning a living. I believe they need a religious education which focuses on roles other than roles for materialistic gain. They need opportunities to discuss their individual purposes in their day-by-day behavior. They need to cycle through their many options and make decisions for themselves about the roles they will play in our society.

12-15 Years—Role Playing

Judgments based on intentions are possible at this developmental level. Therefore, religious education should challenge the early adolescents to choose behavioral goals with the consequences of their behavior in mind. Even though they tend to be clannish and conformist, they can begin to consider the effects of their behavior and their group's behavior on other people. Role playing is an effective technique to use.[3]

6-11 Years—Learning with a Purpose

Whenever children set goals for their behavior in church school or home, they are learning to be purposeful. Gradually they can begin to learn the effect of their behavior on others. Helpers for God can be translated at a concrete level to such goals as, "I will take turns at the playground" or "I will help Brendan rake the leaves." These goals may not sound like much. However, these are steps along the way for the learners to ultimately learn the value of "Purposeful Behavior."

Purposeful roles for action at this developmental level suggest to me that the area of worship deserves attention. I have seen children herded into the front pews of church and threatened to behave or else. I think an opportunity in religious education is wasted. The children should be learning the actions, behaviors, of worship. Teach the children what to do during prayers, what to do during the hymns, and so forth. As reading abilities improve teach them to join in the responses, reading the psalms, and the creeds with the rest of the congregation. Give them appropriate behaviors by modeling and by training so that worship is meaningful as they actively participate.

2-5 Years—Playing with a Purpose

Spiritual Guidance

Christian Maturity

Mature Christians may seek counsel from other persons. But, ultimately, it is the guidance of the Holy Spirit which sustains them.

16-28 Years—Guidance from Mentors

These young people have achieved Selman's stage of Autonomous Interdependence in social relations. They are at one of Tiedeman's Implementation stages in career decision making. Their Idealistic Feelings involve others' as well as their own ideas. In the midst of planning the rest of their lives, they may forget that guidance can come, not only from school counselors, personnel workers in college, employment counselors, and employers, but also from God. Education in prayer should be an important part of religious education for this developmental level.

The mentor relationship is worth mentioning.[4] It is common for young people in their twenties to attach themselves to a mentor (a sponsor, teacher, advisor, or counselor). Religious educators should consider for themselves a loving mentor role for young people. The mentors role commonly lasts only 2-8 years. But it can be important as a step toward Spiritual Guidance.

12-15 Years—Guidance from Community

These early abstract thinkers need to deal with the concept of God with their new cognitive structures. Whether or not they will be ready to ask God for guidance is questionable, although they should have opportunities in worship and prayer. What I do think they need are mature adults in their faith community who are respected and respecting to whom they may turn for guidance. I think religious educators have an awesome responsibility to early adolescents for modeling God's love and caring. They need adults over and beyond their cherished peer group.

6-11 Years—Guidance from Authority Figures

Children are accustomed to turn to parents, teachers, and other adults for guidance. God is an authority figure. However, their prayers are apt to be "my will be done" rather than "Thy will be done." Elkin's research findings indicate that prayer for younger elementary-school children is something outside themselves while the older children individualize and perceive prayer as coming from within and as their talking to God.[5] Late elementary-school children can be helped to see prayer as asking for guidance. They probably cannot fully comprehend the concept but the first steps can be taken to approximate the comprehension in preparation for future development.

2-5 Years—Guidance from Parents

Courage with Learning

Christian Maturity

Mature Christians have the courage to continually learn and witness.

16-28 Years—Courage to Continue Learning

Late teenagers are too often turned off by school learning. Too often they are justified because they must submit to teachers who are authoritarians. This is a shame because with their new cognitive abilities and their capacity for complexities, they should be recycling to new levels of learning. For young adults entering the job market, social pressures to conform to adults who too often are at less mature levels of development wins the day and the courage to learn is denied. Religious educators can provide a welcome climate for continued learning of things religious.

12-15 Years—Persistence

Early adolescents generally are eager to learn social skills even though it takes courage for many. They tend to protect peers and self in a negative manner. Yet they can be challenged to more positive behavior. This is an age group where churches hurt from drop-outs. One reason for dropping out of religious education may be that they are not challenged to use their new cognitive abilities.[6] They may feel that religion is just so much kid stuff. This is a shame because this is the level when formal religious education can begin in earnest. They begin to understand the abstraction of the Bible, the Gospels, church symbols and their heritage. They need to develop the persistence to learn as much as possible. Resource material should be available to them. They deserve a rich cognitive diet.

6-11 Years—Self-Motivated Learning

It seems to me that courage to learn at this level requires two things. First, religious educators can encourage persistence in learning tasks. The learning tasks can be social, cognitive, or self-awareness. They will need help in organizing their tasks and then sticking with each task to completion.

The second area involves their learning on their own, learning to be self-motivated learners. This requires your reinforcement when they do learn on their own. Give them opportunities to try skills on their own. Praise successes. There will be failures and they can also be useful in learning.

2-5 Years—Make-Believe and Real

Wise Decision Making

Christian Maturity

Mature Christians seek the will of God in their decision making. Their decisions are wise because of the high level of complexities dealt with. They judge with freedom of choice.

16-28 Years—Learning to Judge

How can late teenagers and young adults be helped toward wise decision making? They must be given opportunities to make their own judgments without pressure from so-called authorities. They must become their own authorities released from self by freedom in Christ. They will need the support, love, and encouragement from a Christian community as they try to deal with complexities and often fail. Their value education is surely a long-term process.

12-15 Years—Learning Decision Making Skills

When you see this developmental level as a buffer zone between childhood and adulthood, you can appreciate some of the ramifications of this interaction from the Group Model. Young adolescents are not yet ready to make a career decision. They may make a religious commitment but it will be immature. I think the religious educator's role is to respect the buffer zone and not press for final decisions. They will not be free choices in a mature sense. Challenge them to continue to explore what they think and how they feel about religion. In the meantime, teach them the skills of decision making.

6-11 Years—Concrete Choices

Most of these children's choices will have to do with day by day experiences in the groups in which they are learning to operate. The choices are based on a concrete outlook where the alternatives are black or white. "Do I break the rule (black) or follow the rule (white)?"

Religious educators can help these children by providing them opportunities to make choices. Moreover, teachers can help the children begin to seriously consider the consequences of their decisions. Learners must learn to be responsible for their choices. This is a good age in late elementary school to let them live with consequences. This is a method for helping them understand norms and understand the groups to which they belong.

2-5 Years—Loving Choices

Refer to following section.

Summary

We have looked at the seven Philosophy interactions in a step by step, backward progression. This is one way to approach the educational system I am promoting. My brief descriptions of interactions at developmental levels were suggestions to religious educators about what I think is appropriate in values education. I realize that a developmental bias is apparent. I also realize that a developmental approach is not always correct. For example, an early religious experience can be life-shaping as can be a teenage conversion.[7] Nonetheless, I have chosen a developmental, educational system as the best way to approach religious education for most learners.

Another way of viewing the educational system I am proposing for values education is to look at one developmental level across all seven interactions from the Group Model. I have reserved the Preschool level in order to illustrate.

Preschool Values Education

I have written about religious education for preschool children extensively elsewhere.[8] Therefore I will look at the interactions of the Group Model only briefly.

First let us look at some titles for developmental stages for 2-5 year olds.

Title	Theorist	Type of Development
Heteronomous	Dupont	Affective
Intuitive Affects	Piaget	Affective
Preoperational	Piaget	Cognitive

Title	Theorist	Type of Development
Egocentric	Selman	Interpersonal
Love	Maslow	Needs
Impulsive	Loevinger	Ego Development

Next I am going to list the seven interactions from the Group Model and alongside them give you titles that might apply for the preschool developmental level. In other words, the title on the right hand side is related to the title on the left hand side as an appropriate step that can be taken during the preschool period. They approximate progress possible in preparation for the elementary age level in the long progression during a lifetime toward ultimate goals in values education.

Ultimate Goals	Preschool Goals
Perceiving Talents Objectively	Discovering Talents
Self-Acceptance	Self in Family and Playgroup
Intentional Vocation	Fantasizing Life Goals
Purposeful Behavior	Playing with a Purpose
Spiritual Guidance	Guidance from Parents
Courage with Learning	Make-Believe and Real
Wise Decision Making	Loving Choices

Discovering Talents—Preschool children need to feel good about their achievements. This is the basis for intrinsic conditioning which eventually leads to a self-motivated learner.

Self in Family and Playgroup—Self in family comes first.

Then the beginnings appear for self in playgroup as egocentricity wanes.

Fantasizing Life Goals—Fantasy play in the preschool years is the flowerbed out of which creativity blossoms. Fantasy should be encouraged in these impulsive youngsters. Fantasy enriches lives and can contribute eventually to vocation.

Playing with a Purpose—Play is work for preschoolers because it is such an important part of learning. It is the purposefulness that needs to be encouraged in these impulsive children.

Guidance from Parents—Little children look to their parents to guide them. Parents who look to God for guidance model a mature religion for those intuitive children.

Make-Believe and Real—Most preschool children cannot distinguish between make-believe and real. They can be helped to make the distinction only when their make-believe buffer zone is no longer needed. Having made the distinction, care should be exercised that they recognize that both are important. It is not either/or; it is make-believe *and* real.

Loving Choices—Preschoolers who have their basic needs filled and also have their love needs met can begin to reciprocate with loving behaviors of their own. First they learn to please their parents. Then they begin to learn about being loving with playmates and others.

An Educational System

Seven interactions for five developmental levels is the scaffold for an Educational System. This can be seen in

Table IX. You can read down a column as we did for all seven interactions, or you can read across a row as we just did at the Preschool level. It represents a complete system.

Inasmuch as the Group Model represents a whole, integrated personality, the 7 × 5 matrix in Table IX represents a whole learner from childhood to maturity for the element Philosophy.[9] I propose that Philosophy best approximates the ultimate goals of religious education in a Group Model where the original elements can be traced back to the Sermon on the Mount. Lacking that history in the development of this Group Model, the theoretically dictated interactions still have power that is strengthened by the history.

The concept behind the 7 × 5 matrix in Table IX is a theoretical approach to building curriculum. My titles for the thirty-five cells are tentative and are built on knowledge of developmental levels plus experience with the Group Model interactions.[10] Nonetheless, the concept is powerful because of its usefulness. Any educational system which purports to address the whole learner, needs a straightforward method of evaluating success (or lack of it). Values education deals with ambiguities as we have seen. However, any educational system can be checked against the Group Model to insure or rule out inclusiveness. The question, "Does the educational system include all interactions?" can be solved.

The same can be said for a curriculum specific to a developmental level. The term "project" is common. Does the "youth project" include all the interactions? This can be checked. If all seven interactions are not present, do we want to add something to the project? Or do we want to admit an incompleteness and be sure to include unaddressed interactions in a following project?

Table IX. An Educational System for Values Education which Covers the Life Cycle and the Seven Group Model Interactions for an Integrated Philosophy

	EoX	SoW	VoM	AoR	GoH	CoL	JoD
Mature	Perceiving Talents Objectively	Self-Acceptance	Intentional Vocation	Purposeful Behavior	Spiritual Guidance	Courage with Learning	Wise Decision Making
16–28 yrs.	Evaluating Objectively	Autonomy of Self in Society	Identity in the Career World	Actions for a Purpose	Guidance from Mentors	Courage to Continue Learning	Learning to Judge
12–15 yrs.	Learning Evaluation Skills	Identity in Peer Group	Beginning Abstraction of Life Goals	Role Playing	Guidance from Community	Persistance	Learning Decision-Making Skills
6–11 yrs.	Perceiving Talents of Self and Others	Identity in School	Concretizing Life-Goals	Learning With a Purpose	Guidance from Authority Figures	Self-Motivated Learning	Concrete Choices
2–5 yrs.	Discovering Talents	Self in Family and Play-group	Fantasizing Life-Goals	Playing With a Purpose	Guidance from Parents	Make-Believe and Real	Loving Choices

I want to conclude by illustrating from an ongoing religious education practice what I am talking about. I will have to inspect either projects or age-level curriculum rather than entire educational systems.[11]

Maria Harris teaches a semester course each year called "The Aesthetic and Religious Education" at the Andover Newton Theological School.[12] Her hope for her course is maturity and integration for her students. While not really condemning "the over-reliance on psychology in our century,"[13] she feels the necessity of adding aesthetic or artistic development in considering maturity. Since my book is heavily biased in favor of developmental psychologists, it would appear that a fair test of what I have done with the Group Model of Personality Integration is to check Harris' course for the seven interactions for an integrated Philosophy. Beyond that fair-test criterion, I would want to add another criterion. I have approached values education in a straightforward manner, a logical step at a time. That is a normal research procedure. It is an analytical, left-lobe procedure. Maria's course approaches religious education quite differently. I hesitate to name it a right-lobe approach. Hoever, the aesthetic dimensions of religious education suggest intuition, creativity, and making meaning in ways that are not analytical or rational.[14] Can the Group Model and what I have done with it be helpful to a Maria Harris? Or to state it the other way around, will the Group Model and what I have done with it be validated by the Harris course in aesthetics? Each comes from an entirely different background. Can the Group Model transcend such differences? I believe the Group Model has this power.

First, I want to give you an overview of Maria's course. Then, I want to get down to specifics which are illustrations of the seven interactions we have dealt with in this chapter and chapter 11. Remember that her students are young and middle-aged adults who are bent on learning theology and/or religious education. Maria defends her course as not the "only course" but "an essential course, precisely because of this integrating, holistic, and digesting quality. It provides an oasis where people can, in stillness, let their understanding, their intellect, and their feeling come together without pressure, but with support from within the institution where they are learning."[15]

Students meet for a two-hour session once a week. Each student is required to explore an unknown art field and be prepared to present and then help others in the class engage in the particular art field—a real hands-on adventure. The media may be clowning, puppetry, weaving, painting, dancing, cooking, whatever elicits a creative, artistic mode of communicating in other than a discursive, serial mode. She recommends a "presentational symbolism" which is a "simultaneous, integral presentation," "made all at once."[16] An aesthetic form can do this in art in ways no verbal communication can.

I have described briefly what happens in class sessions. Beyond this, a brief overview should include other aspects of her course. Reading is assigned. Term papers are a concluding requirement. An outdoors-in-nature experience is included. Silences are treasured. I will refer to more specifics as we explore the seven interactions from the Group Model.

Perceiving Talents Objectively. I would say that this interaction is an integral part of Maria's course. The students are urged to explore talents which may have been buried in childhood. For example, painting which may have been clumsy in childhood and, unfortunately, frowned upon by adults, now becomes a joy and release for the spirit. As class members present their new-found media, each is critiqued and each in turn critiques the others. This, surely, is training in "Perceiving Talents Objectively."

Self-Acceptance. Attention to aesthetics adds a new dimension for students accustomed to textbooks, lectures, exams, and cognitive content. This new dimension gives them a breather, so to speak, and allows them space to get closer to their own particular place in our world. Harris describes four wisdoms which she hopes are end products for her students: foolishness, creativity, wholeness, and worship. She has evidence from term papers that all four wisdon's are found in her students.[17] All four are important for "Self-Acceptance."

Intentional Vocation. By reason of self-selection (students choose to go to Andover Newton Theological School), the students in Harris' class are already motivated for a calling. Without more information about her course, I have no way of judging the existence or absence of this interaction in the course except by inference. By adding the aesthetic dimension to their lives, Harris' students enlarge their vision of how they can best carry out their vocation. Perhaps, too, their ministry to others in their futures will include sharing artistic forms in some way analogous to their experiences in this course.

Purposeful Behavior. This interaction, of course, is built into any academic course if students want to receive an honorable grade. However, remember that the interaction is between the elements, Action and Roles. To even pass the course, students must sometimes take on new roles for a purpose and then purposefully so direct their actions to perform in these roles. Their gain from Purposeful Behavior is, of course, a gain in their creative wisdom.

Spiritual Guidance. The fourth wisdom Maria Harris speaks of is worship. She says, "Although the course is not a course on or about worship, it steals into the curriculum each year."[18] Again, I must hesitate because her students have selected education in a theological school. As with the Intentional Vocation interaction, I do not know enough about Maria's course to pass judgment on this interaction. I would guess that the interaction is there strongly because I suspect that Harris is a mentor to her students.

Courage with Learning. I have followed the original ordering of the seven interactions faithfully, not because I wanted to, but because of continuity and conformation in writing style. When I first read about the course *The Aesthetic and Religious Education,* I thought about the "Courage with Learning" interaction. Maria's students talk about risk as they try out new learnings. Then they are called on to perform before the class. I would be terrified in such a class. Only by great effort could I persist and learn in order to perform as a clown, let's say, and then dare to get my classmates to also make such fools of themselves (the wisdom of foolishness). Harris' course is grounded in this particular interaction.

Wise Decision Making. The students undoubtedly gain in this value. They learn to appreciate the aesthetic, the creative, the intuitive in their judgments. Decision making is unhurried. Reflection is encouraged. I agree with Maria Harris that adding the aesthetic dimension is a necessity in religious education. It adds joyfulness to the complexities we must daily deal with and it adds a spiritual depth. The aesthetic dimension rounds out religious education and makes religious education whole.

The aesthetic dimension course at Andover Newton rounds out this book. I can end artistically. We have talked about values and how to teach values. Then I gave you seven Christian values and an educational system from the Group Model with suggestions for how to teach those seven Christian values. Finally, we were fortunate enough to find a course in aesthetics where those seven Christian values are being taught today.

Chapter 12 Notes and References

1. I believe that religious education begins at birth, not at two years of age. I know that all through this chapter I run the risk of chronologically categorizing people. This I would hate to do. Individual people cannot be set into sterile cells based upon their age. I insert ages only as a guideline. The stage in development is what is important. Religious educators should assess where each learner is in development in order to effectively plan learning procedures.

2. Throughout this chapter my titles are tentative. Someone else with more insight may create different titles that are more effective.

3. I am using role playing as defined by Hilgard, "A method for teaching principles affecting interpersonal relations by having the subject assume a part in a spontaneous play." see Ernest R. Hilgard, *Introduction to Psychology* (New York: Harcourt, Brace and World, 1962).

4. Daniel J. Levinson, *The Seasons of a Man's Life* (New York: Ballantine Books, 1978), pp. 97–101.

5. David Elkind, *The Child's Reality: Three Developmental Themes* (Hillsdale, N.J.: Lawrence Erlbaum, 1978).

6. A. Rodger Gobbel speaks of challenging and facilitating formal thinking with adolescents in "Christian Education with Adolescents: An Invitation to Thinking," *The Living Light* 17 (2) (Summer, 1980).

7. See autobiographical chapters in *Modern Masters of Religious Education,* ed. Marlene Mayr (Birmingham, Ala.: Religious Education Press, 1983), particularly those by Donald M. Joy, James Michael Lee, and John H. Westerhoff III.

8. Lucie W. Barber, *The Religious Education of Preschool Children* (Birmingham, Ala.: Religious Education Press, 1981).

9. Actually, one interaction has been omitted. The element Uniqueness is the identity element in the Group Model. As the Identity element, it is neutral.

10. These developmental levels are gross. They can be usefully subdivided and assessment devices constructed for developmental stages within each of the cells. This is what I did for the seven interactions for Self in the *Barber Scales of Self-Regard: Preschool.*

11. Copyright laws and space prohibit testing a whole educational system.

12. The course is described by Maria Harris in *Aesthetic Dimensions of Religious Education,* ed. Gloria Durka and Joanmarie Smith (New York: Paulist Press, 1979), chapter 10.

13. Ibid., p. 143.

14. Recall Lazarus' work described in chapter 7.

15. *Aesthetic Dimentions in Religious Education,* p. 145.

16. Ibid., p. 147.

17. The questions concern students contributions to the course, the contributions of the course to themselves, and the relationship between the aesthetic and religious education.

18. Ibid., p. 150.

Index of Names

Index of Subjects